Will You Hold Me?

"A GLANCE UPWARD AT THE EXTENDED ARMS
OF CHRIST RENEWS MY INNER STRENGTH
AND ENCOURAGES ME TO BE AN EXTENSION OF
HIS ARMS TO MY CHILDREN."

Dan Seaborn

Will You Hold Me?

and other devotional thoughts for parents of young children.

Sunday mornings and other weekly events create false images of our families. No one sees the war over which dress your four-year-old will wear to church and whose turn it is to sit in the front seat. We've trained them to look good, keep their noses clean, say "Yes, Ma'am" and pay attention in class. But . . . after church is over it's back to the war zone where pajamas are yet to be put away, lunch is not served quick enough, well . . . you know!

Joseph and Mary were no exception to this challenging thing called family life. Luke 2:41-50 recounts a moment when they were looking for their Son who appeared to be lost in the crowds. When they finally found Him, Mary expressed her surprise that Jesus had put them through those anxious moments. Though she had held the King of Kings in her arms, she often needed someone to hold her. God supplied that need by giving Joseph and Mary strength and direction for the responsibility of parenting.

I trust these devotional thoughts will bring you a few laughs and a few tears and will remind you of the fact that God holds us as we "train our children in the way they should go, so when they are old they won't depart from it."

Dedication

My family is the joy of my life. Jane, thank you for the love
and dedication you give to me every day. Alan, Joshua, Cristina
and Anna Elizabeth, I love you and commit myself to being a
mentor of God's love to you. Through Christ, you are the
inspiration for all I do. Thanks for being my family.

Table of Contents

Will You Hold Me?

Theme:
The comfort of God's loving arms.
Text:
Deuteronomy 33:27

*"The eternal God is your refuge, and underneath are
the everlasting arms."*

At a theme park or a zoo, in a busy hallway, and especially after a tiring day, I'm sure you've heard these words: "Daddy . . . Mommy . . . please hold me." Your child's arms reach high and the look on her face shows an inner hope that only you can fulfill. You reach down with arms of love and clutch your little one. Her head gently presses against your shoulder, signifying trust and security.

I hold my hands up, too. In moments of insecurity, tiredness or fear, I ask Jesus if He will hold me. His willingness never subsides. His mercy is new every morning. He continues to amaze me with the assurance and comfort He provides.

Being held provides comfort. Deuteronomy 33:27 illustrates this thought so clearly: "The eternal God is your refuge and underneath are the everlasting arms." There are times I feel so inadequate as a parent. I get tired and depressed; I overbook my schedule and misplace my priorities. I plod along, looking for comfort and security — someone to give me strength and hope. A glance upward at the extended arms of Christ renews my own inner strength and encourages me to be an extension of His arms to my own children.

I recall the words of a familiar chorus:

> We are His hands, we are His feet,
> We are His people, children of the King!

Our children need to see His loving arms extended through us. We are the ones who can hold them through their stages of learning and questioning. We are the ones who can teach them about the everlasting arms of the Lord.

Consider these three ways we must learn to hold our children:

- Hold them **spiritually** through prayer, devotions and godly guidance.
- Hold them **physically** to give them strength, comfort and help.
- Hold them **emotionally** to provide constancy through all the changes in their lives.

Parenting Points:

List specific ways you can help your children in each area:

Spiritually:
1.

2.

3.

Physically:
1.

2.

3.

Emotionally:
1.

2.

3.

Prayer:

Lord, we accept the responsibility of being Your arms to our children.
As You hold us, so hold our children in Your everlasting arms.
Use us to bring glory to You. Amen.

I Cried a Tear

Theme:
Crying . . . a gift of emotion.
Text:
John 11:35

"Jesus wept."

Disney pictures tear me up. Maybe it's because I don't expose myself to many movies, but the result of watching those animated flicks is always the same. I usually cry five or six times during the film and my children say, "Dad, what's wrong?" I respond with sputtered words about how touching it is and how it reminds me of my own childhood. Those animators and writers know how to get at my inner emotions.

I cry when I listen to elderly people talk about their memories. A gentleman in our church, fondly known as Grandpa Gary, shared his wonderful eighty-two years of life with his family. He told about the joy of his children and recalled their toddler days. Those of us gathered around were touched by his tears as he stressed the importance of training them up to follow Christ. We laughed at some of the experiences and changes he had faced over the years. The fact that he once owned the prominent gas station in town and was a successful businessman didn't matter. In his own words . . . "These children God allows me to love are all that really matter." His words struck a sensitive chord in my own heart. I cried openly as Grandpa Gary continued recalling memories of his life and building memories in mine.

Christ himself wept openly. His emotion came from memories of His dear friend and godly brother, Lazarus. He also was touched by the love He saw in Mary and the other mourners. In this moment, overcome with emotion, Jesus was not ashamed to let His tears be seen.

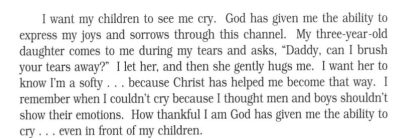

I want my children to see me cry. God has given me the ability to express my joys and sorrows through this channel. My three-year-old daughter comes to me during my tears and asks, "Daddy, can I brush your tears away?" I let her, and then she gently hugs me. I want her to know I'm a softy . . . because Christ has helped me become that way. I remember when I couldn't cry because I thought men and boys shouldn't show their emotions. How thankful I am God has given me the ability to cry . . . even in front of my children.

Parenting Points:

Are you teaching your children the value of allowing tears to flow? What hinders you from being open and honest with your hurts?

Share with your spouse and family some experiences that have been painful and how crying helped you deal with the issues.

Prayer:

Lord, thank You for understanding our hurts and needs.
Continue to give our family guidance and help us use the emotions
You have given us to deal with our pain. Thank You for being an
example in all areas of life, even in tears. Amen.

Stay in the Backyard!

Theme:
Keeping your children within God's boundaries.
Text:
Ephesians 6:2-3

"'Honor your father and mother' — which is the first commandment with a promise — 'that it may go well with you and that you may enjoy long life on the earth.'"

Pets are easy to keep in the backyard. With the newest technology, a laser can be pointed across your lawn and if your pet strays beyond the limit of that laser, his collar will give him the shock of his life. My friend, Jim, recently took his dog for a ride in the car but forgot to turn off the laser. When the car reached the boundary of their invisible fence, the shock collar engaged and his dog went into a frenzy in the car. Of course he quickly turned off the shock system and spared the dog further pain.

What a great help this system would be for parenting! Imagine God creating us with a built-in shock collar that keeps us in His will.

Some friends of mine could have used such a system recently when, for the first time, they experienced the rebellion of their fifteen-year-old son. This child had never given them any trouble. When the discipline problems surfaced, they shook their heads in disbelief. "We didn't think we would ever have to face this," they said.

This is a great reminder for all of us. We must not think we've reached a point of relaxing in parenting. Just as we can never take our eyes off the two-year-old in the backyard, we can never take our eyes off the needs of the teenage years.

Our little children do not grasp the concept of "honoring their parents in the Lord." That is a concept we are to teach to our children so they will have the rewards of long life in Christ. When we teach eternal principles, they become permanent marks on the minds of our children. If the teenage years bring great trials, our comfort can be found in the fact that we have given God's Word to our children.

Parenting Points:

What are you doing to establish spiritual backyard boundaries for your children?

Do you discipline yourselves to live in God's backyard? If not, where are you straying and what will you do to correct your behavior?

Prayer:

Lord, as we establish the backyard, give us guidance.
Help us know when and how to choose our battles.
Protect us with Your lasers of love. Amen.

20
Questions

"The Lord sets prisoners free."

You've probably played the game. You try to name the item someone is thinking of by asking 20 questions. Can you hold it? Is it bigger than a bread box? (We've changed bread box to microwave.) Can you eat it? Is there one in the house? Is it alive? These and many more questions are asked until they tally up to 20. After all the questions, everyone in the family gets to guess what the item is. The one who guesses it first gets a prize. We like to play it during those long, killer car rides.

As parents, we are constantly involved in another game of questions. "Can I go to Bob's party?" "Why is that a bad word?" "If they do it, why can't I?" "Did you do it when you were my age?" If you haven't faced it yet, it's coming. I want my children to feel free to ask me any question they need answered. Hopefully, with God's help, I will direct them in the right paths of life.

During my college years, I experienced a time when many doubts about God rose in my mind. One professor gave me the freedom to ask any question without threat of punishment. I had not experienced that freedom because I believed it was wrong to question God. It was one of the most liberating moments of my spiritual walk, to know that God understood my development and knew I must face some real issues before I could continue to grow in Him.

As God has set the example for me, now I must set the example for my children. My children will ponder the same questions and wander through the same stages I did, and my wisdom will be reflected in how I respond to their questions about life. Join with me in giving our children freedom to ask without immediate judgment. Not allowing that freedom is the same as making them prisoners in their own minds. Free your children to explore God's love and His plan for them. Be a parent who is willing to listen and help them find the answers.

Parenting Points:

What questions will your children soon be asking that you can pray about now?

Are there any questions you've been negligent in answering for your children?

What tough question is God helping you deal with as parents? In what area do you need His help today?

Prayer:

Father, allow us to seek our answers from You and be willing to listen to the questions of our children. We realize they will deal with problems we don't understand. Give us guidance and wisdom when we can offer no answer, and provide for them during the course of their lives. Bless them with the ability to listen to Your voice. Amen.

Family Hugs

Theme:
The importance of touch.
Text:
Luke 18:15-16

"Let the little children come to me."

I know a family that is a terrific example of the importance of touch. They welcome everyone into their home with open arms. Children especially receive extra hugs to remind them how special they are. No one leaves that house feeling unwanted or unloved.

Our family has begun a practice that is creating the same type of fun in our home. Every now and then someone will say, "Family hug time", and we all fight for the position that appears the middle of the circle. We usually end up kissing each other randomly — with our eyes closed, of course, so we won't be distracted by runny noses and dirty faces. If we go a few weeks without this delightful moment together, I can count on a few complaints from the children.

Christ taught each of us the importance of touch. In His day, it was common for people to bring their children to religious leaders for a blessing. In today's scripture, Luke 18:15-16, Jesus is taking a moment from a business discussion to pick up a few children, give them a hug and bless them on their way. Can you imagine what joy His touch brought to parents of those children? Jesus was a proponent of the family hug. He wanted people to understand the importance of touch and He was willing to make a few disciples mad to get His point across.

Let this be a reminder to some of us to put the phone down or close the lap-top and yell, "FAMILY HUG TIME." Go ahead. Try it! You'll like it, and your children will thrive in the warmth and security of your love.

You've heard all the additional reasons psychologists say we need touch. Add this one to your memory log and start a new fad in your neighborhood. And, say, if opportunity knocks, hug the bully when he's playing in your backyard.

Parenting Points:

How are you appropriately teaching your children the importance of proper touch and hugs?

Are you good role models of proper touch in front of your children? Do you hug at all?

Prayer:

Lord, Your hugs of love have sustained us many times during our Christian walk. Allow our children to see Your love through our touch. Please protect them from those who would abuse them with inappropriate touch. Our family hugs You back. Amen.

Thanks, I Needed That

Theme:
The discipline of our children.
Text:
Proverbs 3:12

"The Lord disciples those he loves, as a father the son he delights in."

Take a second to recall the last time you were wound tightly and ready to snap. Have you ever tried to discipline your children during such a moment?

It always seems to happen to me when I've tucked my children in for the fifteenth time or when they can't talk without whining. If I'm carrying any excess tension from work, it's very easy to lose control of both my voice and my actions.

Nothing keeps me in check on those occasions like a spouse who's a bit more levelheaded. Her affirmation is also a positive motivator because of her own credibility in this area.

Recently at the dinner table, our youngest son took me to that snapping point. I, in control, made my way to his chair and took him to the wobble room (that's what we call our discipline room — there's always a little wobble room to discuss the issue) and proceeded to handle the situation correctly. Later in the evening my wife took time to say, "Babe, you handled that situation beautifully!" She'll never know how those words helped me.

It is often difficult for parents to agree when it comes to disciplining children. It is important to understand each other's values and opinions in this area. Take time to sit down and discuss the purpose of discipline in your family and establish the methods you wish to use. If you can't come to an agreement, together seek a third party to help you establish specific guidelines. Without those guidelines, your children will be frustrated and will eventually rebel against any methods.

After my wife and I went through this process, we agreed to establish a wobble room. Having a separate room — a neutral territory — encourages children to openly share their perspectives and discuss solutions. It's a wonderful way to build their independence and responsibility.

God has a wobble room too. I've been there! It isn't always the greatest of experiences, but I'm thankful He's willing to listen and discipline as necessary. His daily doses of mercy and grace are always extended to our families. We will be even more effective as parents as we grow to understand Him and practice His principles with our own children.

❧

Parenting Points:

❧ What makes you tense and edgy with the children? How can you become less stressed by those things?

❧ How can you be more supportive of your spouse when he or she is disciplining your children?

❧

Prayer:

Lord, we know that our children need loving discipline.
Give us unity in this area as we work with each other to train
our children to respect us and love You. Amen.

On Cruise Control!

Theme:
God's hands on the steering wheel.
Text:
Proverbs 16:9

"In his heart a man plans his course, but the Lord determines his steps."

The following story seems unbelievable, but it really happened. A man in South Carolina was driving down the interstate in his new car. He wanted to test his cruise control, so he set it and lay down to take a nap. Moments later he had a terrific collision. When the police arrived and asked what happened, he said, "I thought cruise control meant the car would drive itself." Unbelievable.

However, I fear this occurs with many families. Too often, parents push cruise control and lean back to relax, allowing their children to speed along down their own path. But there is a better control — Jesus Christ. We must put Him behind the wheel and allow Him to have control of our lives. Only then can we avoid the certain disaster ahead.

In his book, *The Strong Family*, Chuck Swindoll teaches many principles related to how he and his wife learned to compromise with their children. Having God in control often meant there were times when they as parents admitted their own steering had taken the family off course, resulting in a dead end. In order to maintain a strong family, all members must keep their eyes on the road and their hands on the wheel.

Recently a gentleman came to my office for counseling. He had put his life on cruise control for the past eight years, and now his thirteen-year-old wasn't willing to let him put the hands back on the steering wheel. I saw the pain in his face as he agonized over the amount of time he had lost with his son. The story is repeated daily. A glance around our neighborhoods reveals the agony of cruise control families. No time for each other. No time to pray. No time to cherish and love. No time . . . .

The good news for us is the same as that which I shared with the gentleman that day. God invites us to turn the controls over to Him. He knows the road; His grace never ends. Proverbs 16: 9 states, "In his heart a man plans his course, but the Lord determines his steps." How true! We can plan and prepare and keep our eyes on the road and hold relentlessly to the wheel . . . but the Lord must determine our steps, the pathways of life. Let us commit ourselves to Him today.

Parenting Points:

~ What have you done to "stay fresh" as parents, to protect yourselves from living on cruise control?

~ Are you giving these specific areas to God to control:
~ Your work?

~ Your free time?

~ Your desires?

~ Your family?

Prayer:

God, continue to provide wisdom to us as a family. Allow us to give You complete control of our direction in life. If You call us to serve, we desire to follow Your call. We are Your family and our purpose is to honor You with our lives. Amen.

Renriting the 10 Commandments

Theme:
The deception of a collapsing society.
Text:
Exodus 20:3

"You shall have no other gods before me."

Though I don't always agree with Rush Limbaugh, his views often expose weaknesses in our democratic system. Recently he listed several commandments of the religious Left which were recorded in *Dispatches*, July 29, 1994. They certainly remind us of the spiritual warfare that exists in our world and beats a constant drum of deception for our children. Ten of those he listed are:

1. Thou shalt have no other God except thyself; after all, it is thy self-esteem that counts. If thou doth not love thyself, who will?

2. Thou shalt not make any graven image out of any substances which cannot be recycled.

3. Thou shalt not take the name of liberals in criticism.

4. Remember the anniversary of Roe vs. Wade and keep it holy.

5. Honor thy mother. If she is dysfunctional, it's thy father's fault.

6. Thou shalt not kill, except life forms under the second trimester.

7. Thou shalt not commit adultery, unless thou aspirest to high political office, useth a condom or cannot help it.

8. Thou shalt not steal, unless thou art disadvantaged or upset with a jury verdict.

9. Always hide the truth about thyself.

10. Always blame someone else for what thou doest.

I know these are jabs at the left wing, but they do reflect some principles that are forcing their way into the mainstream of today's society. What can we do to stand firm against the demoralization of our children? The best way is God's way. Take time to review with your children God's ten commandments for living. I recently laminated a small business size card with these phrases on it:

Any . . . gods before God? Idols? Name in vain? Restful Sabbaths? Lack of honor for parents? Murder? Adultery? Stealing? False witness? Coveting? REVIEW DAILY.

As you analyze these questions, it becomes obvious that they cover every aspect of life. If we can live our lives by these . . . we win. It's important not to get caught up in the left or right, but rather in Christ.

Parenting Points:

Are you aware of the principles your children are learning at school, at the neighbors' and at the gym? Are you involved in and aware of the environments in each of those areas?

Do your children see you living the Ten Commandments or your own set of rules?

Where do you need to adjust to obey these commands?

Prayer:

Father of all commands, thank You for establishing standards for us. Help us to be obedient and walk faithfully in Your way. Protect our children from Satan's treachery and guide them into relationships which will strengthen their love for You. Thank You for Your faithfulness. Amen.

Common Courtesy

Theme:
Being courteous every day.
Text:
John 4:1-26

"Whoever drinks the water I give him will never thirst."

Wow! I just took a half-hour break to grab a quick burger at McDonald's, and what I witnessed amazed me. From my spot in the drive-through on this dreary, rainy day, I saw a McDonald's employee escorting a young lady into the restaurant. I reasoned this must be his girlfriend. But then he ran across the parking lot to escort two men who were taking their school lunch break to get a bite to eat. Next he helped an elderly lady to her car. All the time he was laughing and smiling and inspiring others to do the same. I turned my head in all sorts of directions to witness these good deeds. He was being courteous to everyone he met. I noticed several others were enjoying his actions. It occurred to me that this should be normal, but it's not! This kind of courtesy surprises us.

Other thoughts began to race through my mind. What about in my own home: Have I shown courtesy there? Do my children notice that I open the door for Mom? Do they see me helping with the dishes? Do they hear me say "please" and "thank you"? Does anyone even notice? Of course they do. As a role model of courtesy on a daily basis, I am teaching my children how God wants us to treat others. My family should witness the incidents such as the one at McDonald's and say, "Dad, that looks like something you would do."

John 4:1-26 tells the story of Jesus' meeting with the Samaritan woman. Notice how His courtesy caused her to respond in like manner. He reached beyond the traditions of His own people, for He dared to speak with a Samaritan, a people despised by the Jews. He asked her for a drink and fully expected her to grant His request out of common courtesy. She showed her respect for Him when she called Him, "Sir."

The way people react to us is due in large part to the courtesy we show them. I saw it happen at McDonald's — common courtesy with a smile can brighten a gloomy day.

Home becomes the place where we bring our tired bodies and our frustrations at the end of the day. It is not always easy to behave in a courteous manner toward the rest of the family. But it is always rewarding, for our children will copy our actions and become courteous themselves. Let's be determined to practice common courtesy every day.

Parenting Points:

🐦 Have you practiced courtesy with your family this week?

🐦 List ways you as a family can improve in this area.

Prayer:

Father God, thank You for sending Jesus Christ to be our example of courtesy on earth. We pray for wisdom to teach our children courtesy and kindness. Give us new opportunities each day to show love to others. In Your name, Amen.

Daddy . . . You Make a Lap?

Theme:
The wonder of children.
Text:
Psalm 145:5

"I will meditate on your wonderful works."

I'm thrilled to be a dad when . . .

- the pitter patter of little feet tells me a hug is coming.
- the screams coming from the trampoline are happy ones.
- I lower the basketball hoop to 6 feet and look like an NBA superstar.
- I catch the bike before it teeters on the first ride.
- I build a sand castle in the van from the sand that's left behind after a day at the beach.
- we have to stop on the bike ride to count the ants in the crack on the sidewalk.
- I can leave my work unexpectedly and show up at a little league game with a pitcher of Kool-aid.
- I stand by their beds as they sleep and thank God for the blessing they are to my life.

My three-year-old daughter, Cristina, eased up to me recently as I worked at my computer. It was evening and she was tired. "Daddy," she said, "can you make a lap for me?" I smiled, pushed my chair away from the desk, and gently lifted her to my lap. It was wonderful. Children are wonderful.

A recent story in *Homiletics Magazine* (July-September 1994), tells of a father and daughter who were flying cross-country from New York to Los Angeles. The little girl kept looking out the window exclaiming: "Daddy, Daddy, there's a river . . . Look, Daddy, there's a farm . . . and a barn. Daddy, Daddy, look at that hill down there . . . and there's a beautiful pond with all sorts of ducks on it." The father was busy reading a book, and kept repeating, "uh, huh, uh, huh," until he became a little irritated, then embarrassed by his daughter's excited chatter. Finally he turned to the passengers seated nearby and apologized, "Please forgive my daughter. She still thinks everything is wonderful."

Do you still think everything is wonderful? Are you living wonderfully? Are you full of the joy God offers you? Have you discovered the beauty that surrounds you each day? Have you recently sat still in God's lap, surrounded by His creation?

Our text encourages us to meditate on the wonders He puts before us: His earth, our children, and His salvation. Take a few moments to quietly reflect on His blessings.

Parenting Points:

✒ Do you live life to the fullest and pass on to your children the joy and wonder you possess in Christ?

✒ How often do you get excited about life? If you don't, why? What can you do to change?

Prayer:

God, You are wonderful. Your works are wonderful. Our children are wonderful. We stop to meditate on the wonder of life. Amen.

Don't Backtalk Me!

Theme:
Incorrect responses to God.
Text:
Isaiah 45:9

"Woe to him who quarrels with his Maker."

I was enjoying my meal in Wendy's when a young boy's voice loudly penetrated the air with these words, "I'm not gonna eat this junk. Take me somewhere else." The parents of this little terror soon revealed his problem — THEM!!! They told him to sit quietly while they finished their meal and then they would take him anywhere he wanted to eat. This did not meet with his approval and soon the air was filled with embarrassing statements. In response, the parents took no disciplinary measures and only promised him more rewards for being quiet.

This was an obvious case of poor parenting. Parents who allow their children to talk back are more embarrassing than the children themselves. To help keep from facing a similar embarrassing scenario, here are several helpful hints:

- Discipline privately and quickly. Do not wait or you'll probably let it go.
- Point out to your child his wrongdoing. Be specific and use it as an opportunity to teach.
- Share with your child how you were or weren't disciplined for backtalking and how it affected your life.
- Explain how Christ disciplines us for our actions that are contrary to His will.
- Believe in the child and give him another opportunity.

Isaiah 45:9 records a strong announcement from God. "Woe to him who quarrels with his Maker." To quarrel is to contradict, or in a sense, to backtalk God.

"Woe" means that God's discipline is inevitable. As parents we are responsible for teaching and disciplining our children just as God teaches and disciplines us.

Parenting Points:

In what ways has God disciplined you?

In which areas of your life do you "backtalk" God?

What personal benefits have you received from God's discipline?

How can you teach what you have learned to your children?

Prayer:

God, we commit this day to You. We accept what You have for us and seek Your discipline in our lives. We know You have a plan for our family and You will gladly guide us along the path. Forgive us for the occasions we have "backtalked" You. We desire to grow together! Amen.

The Eyes Have It

Theme:
Correction for our spiritually impaired vision.
Text:
Luke 11:33-36

Therefore, if your whole body is full of light, and no part of it dark, it will be completely lighted, as when the light of a lamp shines on you."

How are your eyes? Are you near-sighted or far-sighted? Do you wear corrective lenses? In today's passage from scripture, Jesus taught about spiritual eyesight. It is really quite simple. The eye is the window to the soul. If we allow God's light to shine in our eyes, our whole being will radiate with His goodness. If we focus our eyes on Satan and the forces of evil, then we will be filled with darkness.

This passage takes on more significance as we apply what we now know about the eye. Optometrists have learned there are basic eye disorders which can lead to imperfect vision. There are spiritual applications for each disorders.

MYOPIA (near sightedness) — an inability to focus clearly on distant objects. Families impaired with spiritual myopia have lost sight of their spiritual destination — heaven — because they are so caught up in the worries of today.

HYPEROPIA (far-sightedness) — an inability to focus on objects that are close by. This shows up in our families when we clearly see the faults of others, but overlook the areas in our own lives which are less than perfect.

PRESBYOPIA (aging condition) — a deterioration of the eye caused by the passing of time. Without proper check-ups, our family relationships can suffer from presbyopia which causes them to lose the fervor and joy that once motivated and inspired us.

ASTIGMATISM (out of balance) — the inability to focus on entire images. Astigmatism occurs in our families when we make decisions that go against God's commands. Unwillingness to see the whole picture and listen for God's voice in every situation causes us to be out of balance.

If any or all of these conditions are evident in your family, consider these corrective measures.

⚘ Have regular checkups. Make sure your family is being exposed to God's Word on a regular basis.

⚘ If necessary, use corrective lenses. The cure for your poor spiritual eyesight is within your grasp. Put it into practice!

⚘ Get proper rest. Nothing relaxes your tired eyes like a good rest. Maybe your family needs a time of rest and relaxation together to restore your eyesight. If so, plan for it.

⚘

Parenting Points:

⚘ Share with your spouse a spiritual disorder which affects your life. Pray together for healing and restoration.

⚘ Establish some new ways your family can keep its spiritual vision sharp.

⚘

Prayer:

Lord, You have opened our eyes to the light of Your Word.
Help us as we seek to be healed of our poor spiritual vision.
Thank You for Your faithfulness. Amen.

Count Your Blessings, Name Them One by One

Theme:
The blessing that we are to others.

Text:
Genesis 12:2-3

"I will make your name great and you will be a blessing. . . . and all peoples on earth will be blessed through you."

We live in a "give me" world. It is easy to forget that we should be seeking after that which we can give away for the benefit of others. In their book A Taste of Heaven, Lionel Blue and June Rose relate the following illustration.

A Parable of Heaven and Hell

There was a rabbi who wanted to see both heaven and hell. The rabbi found himself before a door which bore no name. He trembled as he saw it open before him into a room where all was prepared for a feast. There was a table, and at its center a great dish of steaming food. The smell and the aroma inflamed the appetite.

Diners sat around the table with great spoons in their hands, yet they were shrieking with hunger in this terrible place. They tried to feed themselves and gave up, cursing God. For the spoons God had provided were so long that they could not reach their faces and get the food to their tongues. So they starved because of these spoons, while the dish of plenty lay amongst them. The rabbi knew their shriekings were the cries of hell, and as knowledge came, the door closed before him.

He shut his eyes in prayer, and begged God to take him away from that terrible place. When he opened them again, he despaired, for the same door stood before him, the door that bore no name. Again it opened, and it gave onto the same room. Nothing had changed, and he was about to cry in horror. There was the table, and at its center the steaming bowl, and around it were the same people, and in their hands the same spoons.

Yet the shrieking had gone, and the cries and the curses had changed to blessings. And nothing had changed, yet everything. For with the same long spoons they reached to each other's faces, and fed each other's mouths. And they gave thanks to God.

And as the rabbi heard the blessings, the door closed. He bent down, and he too blessed God, who had shown him the nature of heaven and hell, and the chasm — a hairsbreadth wide — that divides them.

Too often our families reflect the first scene in this story. We are too focused on staying in this comfort zone, even though other members of the family may be suffering. I challenge you to turn the spoons around and allow the members of your family to receive your blessings.

Acts 20:35 states, "It is more blessed to give than to receive." Of course we all believe it, the question is do we practice it? We can.

☙

Parenting Points:

☙ Do you tend to focus too much on your own needs and concerns? What can you do to turn the spoon around and begin feeding others in your family?

☙ How can your children begin to give blessings away even at a young age?

☙ Share Acts 20:35 at a dinner meal. Talk about the blessing you have received and the blessing you have given.

☙

Prayer:

Lord, our lives are a reflection of many blessings. Most of all, we thank You for the blessing of salvation You have provided. At our tables of plenty and even during our moments of sacrifice, remind us of the joy of being a blessing for You. Use this family to bring joy to others. Amen.

Ignoring the Blind Spots

Theme:
The importance of facing tough issues.
Text:
Matthew 15:14

"If a blind man leads a blind man, both will fall into the pit."

My friend Tom Bock, an eye doctor, says every person has a blind spot. If you look straight ahead and move your finger slowly across your area of vision there is a place where your finger will disappear. This occurs because of a small separation in the back of our eye where the optic nerve connects to the brain. In that tiny spot there is no reflection of light. Tom says the reason we don't notice the blind spot is because our minds have been trained over the years to ignore it just as we ignore our nose sticking out in front of our face.

Sometimes we ignore obvious areas of concern in our families, resulting in children who are insensitive to those problems as well. It's a case of the blind leading the blind.

Kenneth D. Filkens humorously depicts the blind spots for us in his article entitled *"THE PIT."*

"A man fell into a pit and couldn't get himself out.

A **subjective** person came along and said, 'I **feel** for you down there.'

An **objective** person came along and said, 'It's **logical** that someone would have fallen down there.'

A **Christian scientist** came along and said, 'You only **think** that you are in a pit.'

A **Pharisee** said, 'Only **bad** people fall into pits.'

A **mathematician** calculated **how** he fell into the pit.

A **rockhound** asked him if any rare **specimens** were in the pit.

A **news reporter** wanted the **exclusive** story on his pit.

A **Fundamentalist** said, 'You **deserve** your pit.'

A **Calvinist** said, 'If you'd been saved, you'd **never** have fallen into the pit in the first place.'

A **Wesleyan** said, 'You were saved and you **still** fell into the pit.'

A **Charismatic** said, 'Just **confess** that you're not in that pit.'

An **evasive** person came along and **avoided** the subject of the pit altogether.

A **self-pitying** person said, 'You haven't seen anything until you've seen **my** pit.'

A **valley girl** said, 'It's really you, **sweets**, it's your decor.'

An **optimist** said, 'Things **could** be worse.'

A **pessimist** said, 'Things **will** get worse.'

A **realist** said, '**That's** a pit.

A **scientist** calculated the **pressure** necessary to get him out of the pit.

A **geologist** told him to appreciate the **rock** strata in the pit.

An **IRS** man asked him if he was paying **taxes** on the pit.

A **county inspector** asked if he had a **permit** to dig in a pit.

A **professor** gave him a lecture on 'The **elementary** principles of the pit.'

And Jesus, seeing the man, took him by the hand and lifted him out of the pit!"

What a powerful illustration of recognizing what we need to do — and doing it. I encourage you to stop ignoring the blind spots and pick yourself and your family up out of the pits.

Parenting Points:

What are the pits you often fall into?

Are you choosing to stay in them because of the blind spots in your own life?

Prayer:

Dear God, thank You for bringing us out of the pit and putting our feet on the ROCK to stay. Help us to recognize and avoid the dangerous spots in the walk of life that would land us in the pit, and keep us ever willing to follow Your path. Keep us in Your care. Amen.

Watch Out . . . He's Gonna Blow!

Theme:
The embers of anger.

Text:
II Timothy 1:6-7

*"For this reason I remind you to fan into flame the gift
of God, which is in you through the laying on of my hands.
For God did not give us a spirit of timidity, but a spirit
of power, of love and of self-discipline."*

Our family recently arrived home after a trip out for dinner. As I normally do in the winter, I went to the wood burner to check on the fire. Through the furnace window I could see the glow of the red embers. A slight opening of the furnace door was all that was needed to ignite the embers into roaring flames.

I must confess, often those embers represent me. A hectic day at work, uncontrollable circumstances, negative attitudes or unkind words can cause glowing embers to build up in my life, and all it takes is some simple phrase to ignite me. Even words that normally make me laugh are trigger words during these times. My children even recognize it. I'll overhear them telling Mom, "Watch out for the lion king (that's me) today."

Second Timothy reminds us of the only embers we should fan into flame. "Fan into flame the gift of God." Paul is encouraging Timothy to carry on the godly heritage he has been given — the gifts of faithfulness, strength and endurance.

My occasional outbursts around the home do not teach those qualities. The challenge for me — and for all of us — is to know when we are easily fanned into flame and be ready with a plan to extinguish the embers.

Here are a few suggestions:

- Pray before you go. When leaving work, take time to kneel and ask the Lord to guide you as you share time with the family. Prayer changes *me*.
- Allow your spouse to say, "You need to get control." If you need to go to another room and be alone for a while, do it.
- Acknowledge your failure to the children. Teach them how to say, "I'm sorry."

When we gather strength from God to extinguish the embers of anger, the flames of God begin to blaze in our daily lives.

Parenting Points:

- When are the times and what are the circumstances that most often "cause you to blow"?

- Prepare a plan of action to counterattack upcoming outbursts.

- What gifts do you have from God that need to be fanned into flame?

- How can you fan each other's flame?

Prayer:

Father of all gifts, allow us to use our gifts to honor You.
When our control is weak, strengthen us and help us to
strengthen each other. Amen.

There's a Monster under my Bed!

Theme:
Taming childhood and adult fears.
Text:
Psalm 23:4

"I will fear no evil, for you are with me."

My son dreamed he was at school, and on this day, Mom never came after school to pick him up. For weeks he feared being left anywhere. He followed us into every room and wanted to hold onto our clothing or our hands. He asked several times a day, "Why did you forget me, Mom?" To my knowledge, we have never forgotten him, nor does he have any reason to believe he will be left behind, but it was a REAL FEAR! It caused great stress in our family and he cried often over the course of several weeks.

Our comfort during this time was the encouragement of other parents who said their children had faced the same childhood fear. However, our greatest comfort was God's Word from Psalm 23:4, "I will fear no evil, for you are with me." We taught our five-year-old that Christ is with us always. When we are afraid, His comfort is still in our heart.

WE NEED THAT ASSURANCE! When life is falling apart, relationships are struggling, the kids have pushed you to the limit, and "monsters are coming from under the bed" . . . FEAR NOT! Our Good Shepherd is faithful, and we His sheep have no need to fear.

Think about it from God's perspective. He does not want us to live our lives in fear of the "monsters." Rather than fear them, God wants us to expose them to Him and allow His wisdom and love to guide us through times of fear.

Parenting Points:

❧ List your personal fears for your family.

❧ Are you allowing fear to motivate some parental decisions you make? If so, pray for trust in God.

❧ List individual family members and their specific fears. Pray for the Lord's protection and deliverance from these fears.

❧ Memorize Psalm 23:4, "I will fear no evil, for you are with me."

Prayer:

Lord, thank You for providing peace in our family. We pray You will continue to protect us and keep us from potentially harmful situations which may come our way. We recognize Your power over fear and we give our family fears to You, individually and corporately. Thank You for Your daily protection. Amen.

Permanent Markers

Theme:
Your family's mark in the world.
Text:
Exodus 7:5

"And [they] will know that I am the Lord."

Browsing through an office supply store, I noticed several types of markers available for sale. I began to think about the kind of marks each one makes and realized that these markers are much like Christian people I have met.

Hi-liters: The hi-liter is a person who likes to be in the spotlight. Behind-the-scenes missions work does not give enough exposure, so don't expect this person to visit shut-ins or work on a service project.

Erasable markers: These people live by their own selfish desires and, if necessary, they erase enough of their tracks to keep others from knowing how they really live.

Invisible markers: These people are like the man who once told me he took the winter off with his Christianity. But in the spring he just let it blossom all over again. What a joke! If a special solution must be used to find the mark you've made for the Lord, then your Christianity is full of deceitfulness.

Fine point markers: People living this lifestyle make the lightest possible mark for Christ. They say they're Christians, but no one at work or in their home knows about it. To them, Christianity is something to be hidden under a bushel.

Bold, permanent markers: These Christians are making a stand for Christ in their neighborhood. They represent truth, kindness, discipline, honesty and integrity.

As I read the story of Pharaoh's encounter with Moses, I am impressed by the kind of mark Moses made. He left no doubt in anyone's mind that God was the Lord. At a time when it would have been convenient to hide in the shadows, he boldly proclaimed God's plan for His people.

Whether I like it or not, my family is leaving its mark on our neighborhood. Is it barely seen, or is it bold and permanent?

Parenting Points:

Which marker identifies you? Your family?

What steps can you take to make sure your family is making the right kind of mark for Christ?

Prayer:

Lord, You have shown us what we need to do to make a permanent mark for You in our neighborhood. Direct us and guide us as we follow You. Help us to make a difference in our world. Amen.

Thanks, Grandma

Theme:
Teaching the next generation about God.
Text:
Psalm 78:1-8

"We will not hide them from their children;
we will tell the next generation."

The letter arrived with perfect timing. I had been sharing with my children the importance of learning the trustworthy deeds of God so they could pass them on to their children. My mom, without being privy to this information, wrote a letter to her grandchildren that arrived two days after that conversation. Part of it stated:

"I pray for and ask God's blessings on your life every day. I feel the great responsibility of being the right kind of mother and grandmother, one who sets an example for her children and grandchildren to follow. So remember, I pray every day that my life will reflect Christ so you will see my example and continue to grow in Him. When I reflect on my life, I feel I'm far behind you dear ones and am thankful you have given me much joy in life. As a grandmother, I want to always be there for you. I promise to only tell God whatever you would want to share privately with me. I pray you can tell I love you deeply. Continue to study to improve in school and smile for Jesus. Keep looking up, children . . . Christ may come today! Love and kisses . . . Mom/Grandma."

My oldest son asked me after reading this letter, "Dad, did you tell Grandma to write that letter?" What a great opportunity to show my children this teaching process in action. They could understand their grandmother's great love for them and her desire for them to continue to grow in their love for God. It was a beautiful teaching time with the children.

Psalm 78:1-8 is a wonderful passage that affirms the importance of teaching the next generation the praiseworthy deeds of the Lord. In verse three, the specific responsibility of teaching is given to the fathers. The continuing verses in this passage detail the results of a home and society that does not faithfully carry out these responsibilities. It is easy to see that this passage is being lived out daily in our communities and neighborhoods. God commands us to turn the tide of corruption and moral collapse.

For those who have no heritage of a godly family, it's not too late to start. For those who have inherited godly principles, be faithful to carry the torch of the Lord. Set a new standard for Christ in your home and neighborhood.

Parenting Points:

ᐁ What are the top three things your lifestyle is teaching your children?

ᐁ Who have been godly examples in your life? What do you see in them that you need to repeat in your family?

Prayer:

Lord, allow us to continue to understand Your trustworthy deeds. Keep us faithful as we teach what we learn to our children and grandchildren. Thank You for allowing us to know Your love and grace. Amen.

Catching Fireflies

Theme:
The joy of seeing God's miracles.
Text:
John 10:32

"I have shown you many great miracles from the Father."

When my brother, Joe, and I were young boys growing up in the foothills of South Carolina, a favorite pastime was using Mom's canning jars for catching fireflies. About dusk we'd begin our assault on the little lights that flickered near the bushes and shrubs surrounding our home. Thirty minutes later our jars were teeming with lightning bugs. Sometimes we'd squeeze the area that lit and smear a streak of light down our faces to imitate our Cherokee Indian ancestors.

The cycle continues. I chased after fireflies with my five-year-old last evening. We used an old canning jar for memory's sake. It took us a while, but by dark we had collected a 40-watt bulb's worth of lightning bugs. As we chased after the insects, Joshua asked the key question, "Dad, how does it do it? How do they light up?" I know there are scientific explanations and I'm sure the encyclopedias in my home would provide those details, but the answer I used satisfied my five-year-old's curiosity. "It's a little miracle of God, Josh. The first book of the Bible tells how God created all the creatures of the earth and placed them on the earth. God made this little insect with a built in flashlight so it could see to fly in the night. Just as we use headlights on our car, this little insect uses taillights to light the way." No more explanation was needed. My son accepted this simple answer because of his trust in God. Simple acceptance . . . God-sensitive. I like that . . . **God-sensitive!**

As my son rounds the edge of the shrub and grasps another insect for the jar, he's not just catching fireflies, he's catching miracles . . . and he believes it!

I also grasp one of God's miracles when I wrap my children around my neck and celebrate childhood. It is easy to take my children for granted, but they truly are miracles. Each one is a gift from God. Daily, on my knees, I should remind myself of their value and place in His kingdom.

In John 10:32, Jesus says to those who do not believe he is the Son of God, "I have shown you many great miracles from the Father." Even after seeing those miracles, the people still wanted to kill Christ. Many people still do not understand that children are indeed miracles. I find it hard to comprehend how they can be so blind.

I want to keep catching fireflies and marveling at the miracles of God. I pray that my neighbors will come to see the wonder of God's great love through the wonder of childhood.

Parenting Points:

List some miracles of God you've seen in your family:

How are you helping your children understand God's miracles?

Prayer:

Lord, I am a miracle. So is each member of my family.
Your gifts of life and salvation are miracles. In this world that has
chosen in many ways to abort You, we give You our lives.
Live through us, Lord. Thank You for Your many blessings. Amen.

The Care Bear Family

Theme:
Principles for becoming a caring parent.
Text:
1 Thessalonians 2:7

"We were gentle among you, like a mother caring for her children."

Paul compared the care he gave the Thessalonians with the care a mother gives her little children. It is a gentle, persistent care that develops character.

In his book entitled *Seven Things Kids Never Forget*, Ron Rose shares the following statistics. Every day in America:

- 3 children die by parental abuse.
- 90 children are taken from parents and placed in foster homes.

Of the 65 million Americans under 18, 22% live in single parent homes and 3% have no parents at all. That 3% amounts to 1,950,000 children.

In the midst of this unraveling society, however, there are millions of parents who care about their children and who take seriously the responsibility of their upbringing. Most of them have found that the following principles are timeless and necessary for raising happy well-adjusted children.

- Be willing to sacrifice some of your immediate desires for the sake of your family.
- Talk openly with your children about difficult issues.
- Learn how to pick your battles — which ones must be fought, and which ones can be let go.
- Find ways to surprise and delight your family.

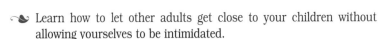

- Learn how to let other adults get close to your children without allowing yourselves to be intimidated.
- Build a team of caring people around them who will support them emotionally, physically and spiritually.
- As your children mature, learn how to let go.
- Celebrate happy days and special events together.
- Be fair in your discipline.
- Tell your children every day about Christ's love for them.

Tender loving care is the one thing so many children are lacking today. Your children will forgive you for all of your shortcomings and most of your mistakes, if only they can be sure that you love them deeply.

Parenting Points:

- Evaluate how you are doing as parents in each of these ten areas.

- Establish a specific time for a family celebration this week.

Prayer:

Caring Father, how we thank You for Your constant care. Be near us as we care for our children, those precious gifts of Your love. Amen.

Let Freedom Ring

Theme:
Teaching our children to respect their heritage and freedom.
Text:
Psalm 119:45

"I will walk about in freedom."

It was a special service honoring D-day. We were reflecting on those soldiers who gave all — even their lives — for our freedom. We stood for a few moments in silence, honoring those who had died for us. Tears began to fill my eyes as I thought what it would be like to lose my own children to war.

Softly, our worship leader began to sing "*My Country 'Tis of Thee.*" The words touched me in a special way. I realize they're not scriptural, but the quality, character, integrity and respect of the words of the hymn gave me a new appreciation for my freedom.

> My country, 'tis of thee, Sweet land of liberty, Of thee I sing:
> Land where my fathers died, Land of the Pilgrims' pride.
> From every mountainside, Let freedom ring.

As we concluded the hymn, I began to wonder how many children today are being taught the value of liberty. Who's telling them about the part Christianity played in founding this country? Who's passing on the heritage of the Pilgrims? These subjects have been delicately brushed away in many of our textbooks. Our children may never know about our Pilgrim ancestors and the many men and women of the armed forces who have risked much to protect our freedom. It is this freedom that allows us to stand with our children and sing to the God of the universe.

The last verse states:
> Our fathers' God, to Thee, Author of liberty, To Thee we sing.
> Long may our land be bright with freedom's holy light;
> Protect us by Thy might, Great God, our King!*

As we sang the last verse, my five-year-old tried to imitate the words coming out of my mouth. I noticed that he was following my example. And then it dawned on me. **I am the one** who must learn to appreciate the devotion of those who have gone before. Because of my example, my children will learn and pass the same values along to the next generation.

Parenting Points:

~ What have you done to teach your children to be thankful for their freedom? What can you do?

~ Take your children to a cemetery and stand by the grave of a soldier who gave his life for our freedom. Pray for this soldier's family.

~ Teach your children the history of the Pilgrims and tell them to share what they learned in their history class.

Prayer:

God of freedom, thank You for allowing us to live in this country. Continue to teach us the value of freedom and give us wisdom to share what we learn with our children. Protect them as they grow and learn of their heritage in You. Allow us to be examples to them in our respect for liberty. Amen.

Hurry up, Let's Go!

Theme:
A slower pace for our lives.
Text:
Psalm 46:10

"Be still and know that I am God."

I sometimes relax and recall the memories of growing up in the slow-paced town of Six Mile, South Carolina. My best friend, Robert, and I would take wheels off old roller skates and try to nail them to boards to make go-carts. Sometimes we'd just make ramps out of the boards and do daredevil stunts with our spider bikes. After tiring of this, we would catch bugs in a canning jar or pick figs off the tree by the old barn. Around noon, mom would call us in for a banana sandwich or a piece of her southern fried chicken. We would wash it all down with sweetened iced tea, and then off we'd go to continue our adventures.

Some days Mom would promise my brother and me a trip to our cousins' swimming pool if we could get the grass cut by lunchtime. We'd take turns running laps with the mower, leaving plenty of uncut grass behind — all in an effort to be swimming by afternoon.

There were many days I spent by myself in Grandpa's barn, looking for dirt dabbler nests and shooting wasps off their nests with my slingshot. My wanderings would take me to the little brook over in the beautiful meadow. It was easy to pass two or three hours turning over rocks and thumping crayfish through the shallow water. Sometimes I found clay in the banks and made pottery jars for Mom. She made me believe they were as good as gold and kept her fancy knickknacks in them.

You get the picture. I had a relaxed life. I had fun. There was time to grow up and learn what being a child was all about. There was time to experience God's beautiful earth without having to explain how it got here and how soon the ozone would be depleted. Though I faced many tough times growing up, I must say it was a great childhood.

Most children aren't getting that opportunity today. By the time they're two, their parents have them in designer jeans and fancy haircuts. Baseball and basketball camps start as soon as they can walk. There's a program that helps them read better so they aren't embarrassed in "preschool." Clothes have all the right logos and sneakers have to be a certain brand.

Why do we do this? Why do we push our children to excel — to do more, see more, have more, be more — at such an early age? Could it be because we parents have not learned how to slow down and relax?

Psalm 46:10 states, "Be still and know that I am God." How long has it been since you have been still long enough to sense His presence and enjoy the world around you? I encourage you to try it today. Take a walk, ride a bike, play a game — relax and enjoy some time with your children. Be still and experience a few moments of peace and tranquility.

Parenting Points:

Find some time today to be still in God's presence.

Are you pushing your children too hard? Are you forcing them to grow up too quickly? What can you do about it?

Prayer:

God, let our home be a place of relaxation — a place where children are allowed to play and have fun and enjoy life. Thank You for Your presence we find in the still and quiet moments of the day. Amen.

The Happy Meal

Theme:
Joyous meal times.

Text:
Luke 22:16

"For I tell you, I will not eat it again until it finds fulfillment in the kingdom of God."

I bet you've tried — as I have — to keep the children distracted while driving past the "golden arches." I think it's impossible. They have an intrinsic ability to detect toys and food close by. And what's with this happy meal stuff? That's a euphemism. Our children fight over who got the green toy and which one is bigger. They hardly even notice there is food in the bag.

Let me tell you what a happy meal is. It's when the whole family sits around the table and shares highlights of the day. It's the mixed laughter of parents and children as we enjoy this time spent together. It's the squeals that erupt when someone drops a chicken leg on the floor and we all scramble to tackle the dog as he runs away with his prize.

Christ talks about a meal like this in Luke 22:16. Here He shares about a time when we will all gather with Him for a meal in the kingdom of God.

Can't you picture that event? We will sit at the table with Christ our Savior and ask Him all the questions that have been burning inside us for so many years. We'll chat with Noah about the ark and ask Daniel about the lion's den. And there will be no end to the joy we will share.

I remember the words of a great hymn, "What a day that will be, when my Jesus I shall see. When I look upon His face, the One who saved me by His grace."

Do your children know about this happy meal? Keep teaching them the principles that will enable them to share in that final feast of joy!

Parenting Points:

- Are mealtimes in your home fun and enjoyable? What can you do to improve them?

- What communication needs to occur at your table? How could it be more uplifting?

Prayer:

Lord, thank You for providing for our family. Every day we ask You to bless our food. We now ask you to bless our mealtimes. Help them to be times of communication and laughter. Create in us a relaxed and peaceful spirit to share with our family. We joyously anticipate a time of sharing with You now and in heaven. Amen.

Heroes

Theme:
The right kind of hero.
Text:
Psalm 48:1

"Great is the Lord, and most worthy of praise."

In one of the last games of his career, Babe Ruth was not doing well. He had struck out each time at the plate. His body seemed to be letting him down. He just couldn't play the game quite like he used to.

He was playing right field. It was the top of the ninth. There were two outs with a runner on second. The score was tied. The ball was hit sharply just to his left. Ruth fielded the ball well, but his throw to third was wild, bouncing over the third baseman's head and allowing the runs to be scored.

The crowd erupted in boos and jeers. They were upset with Ruth for the loss and became unruly toward him.

Suddenly, a little blond-headed boy jumped down onto the top of the dugout and then lowered himself onto the field. As he ran out toward Ruth, a hush fell over the crowd. He jumped up into Babe Ruth's arms and Babe carried the little boy to the dugout. By then the crowd was totally silent.

Later one reporter explained the silence by saying, "The crowd was watching the love of a little boy for his hero, even when his hero failed."

I like to think my children consider me one of their heroes. Through the many failures of my life and the ups and downs of my day, it's great to know there will be squeals of joy and lots of hugs waiting for me when I walk through the front door of my home.

Whether we like it or not, our children look up to us as heroes. They need to have real heroes — men and women who know how to laugh and cry; who are both gentle and strong; who aren't afraid to make mistakes and ask for forgiveness. Our Heavenly Father, who knows us well, can make us into the kind of examples our children need.

Parenting Points:

If your children were asked how their parents deal with failure, what would they say?

Ask God to help you become the right kind of hero for your children.

Prayer:

Lord, thank You for being our Hero. You have protected and cared for us in the game of life. Help us to be godly heroes to our children. Use us to guide their lives toward You. Amen.

Treasure Island

Theme:

Rare and beautiful treasures for God.

Text:

Proverbs 24: 3-4

"By wisdom a house is built, and through understanding it is established; through knowledge its rooms are filled with rare and beautiful treasures."

At my fifth birthday party, one of my cousins gave me a small coin holder that looked like a cat's head. It was bright orange with black whiskers. Stunning? Not really, but over the years, it has been the present I have always referred to as my favorite gift of all time.

Recently, at my mother's home, I was looking through some papers in a drawer, and suddenly, there was my coin holder. It had been 20 years since my hands had last touched it. I cried when I saw it, because it had once been very valuable to me. Clutching it to my chest, I ran to show my children my treasure.

Think back to your childhood. What one gift do you remember as being your "treasure"? Is it still valuable to you? Sometimes we treasure things that really are not that important, thinking that in clutching them to ourselves, we will find happiness.

When I tuck my children in at night, I realize what a treasure God has given me. He has blessed me with happy, healthy children. Is there anything on earth more priceless? What can I do to help them to grow into rare and beautiful treasures I can give back to God?

Proverbs 24:3 states "By wisdom a house is built, and through understanding it is established; through knowledge its rooms are filled with rare and beautiful treasures." What I need are wisdom, knowledge and understanding. And where do I go to find help for my task? I go to the Source of all good things, my Heavenly Father.

With His help, I can make decisions that will be the foundation for our home. As I understand more about His love for me, I can establish loving guidelines for living. And as I increase in knowledge of my world and the One who created it, I can fill my little ones' lives with happy times and treasured memories.

May God help us all to seek those gifts which will lead our children to Him.

Parenting Points:

What kinds of things are you doing with your children that will increase their wisdom, knowledge and understanding?

Memorize Proverbs 24:3-4.

Prayer:

Father, You have blessed our home with rare and beautiful treasures. Give us wisdom and understanding, that we may help our children grow in the knowledge of You. Amen.

Peanut Butter and Jelly

Theme:
Our family's reputation.
Text:
Ephesians 5:15-20

"Be very careful, then, how you live — not as unwise but as wise."

Our family has a reputation. Every family does. The neighbors that live nearby watch our comings and goings and our daily activities, and they talk about us. I wonder what they are saying about my family?

One evening at dinner, the sandwich I was eating fell out of my hand and landed on the table. If it had been a meat sandwich, I would have had to collect all the pieces and put it back together. But it was a peanut butter and jelly sandwich. It stuck together. And then it hit me — I want our family to be like a peanut butter and jelly sandwich. I want us to have a reputation of sticking together no matter what.

Here are three questions we can ask ourselves if we want to evaluate the reputation of our families:

❧ Are you fun to live with?

In the original Greek text the words "be careful" actually read "look very closely at how you live." So look at your life. Ask yourself if you would enjoy living with someone just like you.

❧ Are you fun to grow with?

The growth process can be long and painful. Change does not happen overnight, but with God's help, we can change. We must keep a willing-to-grow spirit alive and vibrant in our homes.

❧ Are you fun to talk to?

Do your children eagerly chat with you about their friends and their day at school? Are they at ease talking with you and with each other? Do you have fun conversations as well as serious talks? There is no substitute for good communication.

These three simple questions are good points for evaluating your family's reputation. Take some time to consider them and begin developing a family that sticks together.

❧ Parenting Points:

❧ Are you fun to live with?
   ❧ Yes, when I'm . . .

   ❧ No, when I'm . . .

❧ Are you fun to grow with?
   ❧ What areas of your life have experienced growth in the last six months?

   ❧ What difference will your growth make in your children?

❧ Are you fun to talk to?
   ❧ What did you talk with your child about this week?

   ❧ Did you listen more or talk more?

   ❧ Can you listen and respond fairly?

❧ Prayer:

Father of unity, thank You for giving us each other. Help us stick together as a family. Give us wisdom and strength and, most of all, love. Amen.

Get Yourself a Logo

Theme:
A theme for life's direction.
Text:
Philippians 4:8

"Whatever is true, whatever is noble, whatever is right, whatever is pure, whatever is lovely, whatever is admirable — if anything is excellent or praiseworthy — think about such things."

Dennis Jackson, a pastor friend of mine, once made a suggestion which my family has put into practice. He recommended that each member of the family adopt a theme word at the beginning of each new year. This was to be a word that would challenge us to do our best in a certain area.

We have experimented with this idea, using it as a way to improve ourselves as well as our family life. My current word is "discipline." In an effort to improve the way he studies and prepares materials for school, our oldest son has adopted "excellence" as his theme word. Our middle son is living with a new "spirit" as his theme. Our daughters are sharing the words "laughter" and "smile." I often ask them what their theme is, and they respond with their word.

Our text from Philippians also suggests several themes for life. They are truth, nobility, purity, admirable, excellence, loveliness. God calls us to think about these characteristics and put them into practice in our lives. In return, God will grant us His peace (v.9).

In His Word God challenges us to follow the example He gave us in His Son, Jesus Christ. We must always be striving to be more like Him, even though we know we will never be perfect. There are many ways to improve our minds, our spirits and our relationships.

Consider adopting a theme word for yourself or for your family. Make it your "logo" — your direction for life. Change your word from time to time so that you will be challenged to grow and mature. Work together and see what happens!

Parenting Points:

⚜ If someone who knows your family were asked to describe you in one word, what would they say? If they were asked to describe you individually?

⚜ What words will you and your family adopt as theme words for yourselves? List them here.

⚜

⚜

⚜

⚜

Prayer:

Lord, by Your example You have taught us about truth, nobility, purity and holiness. Guide our family and help us grow in these areas, as we seek to live according to Your Word. Bless us, we pray. Amen.

Who Left up the Lid?

Theme:
Respect around the home.
Text:
1 Thessalonians 4:12

"Let your daily life win the respect of outsiders."

Every once in a while, this phrase echoes through our home, "Who left up the lid?" Funny, it's never spoken by a male voice. Lowering the lid is such a simple act, yet it's one that is easy to forget. Why is it sometimes hardest to remember to do the simplest acts of kindness? Why do we have to be reminded to take out the trash, clean up the supper dishes and put our dirty clothes in the hamper? Such actions make a statement about our respect for others in the home.

Disrespect for others begins when children are very small. Three-year-olds who refuse to help make their bed become sixteen-year-olds who are unwilling to respect any curfew. We parents much teach respect to our children in the early years.

It would be worth our while to set the example for our children based on the passage in 1 Thessalonians 4:11-12: "Make it your ambition to lead a quiet life, to mind your own business and to work with your hands, just as we told you, so that your daily life may win the respect of outsiders and so that you will not be dependent on anybody."

Note those words, "Make it your ambition." To fulfill an ambition requires effort. This speaks volumes to me as a parent. In order to win the respect of my children, I must put forth an effort. I must teach by example. I must make it my goal to show respect for others — especially in my home. How can I do that? By doing those simple acts of kindness that make life better for everyone.

Consider for a moment our ultimate example, Jesus Christ. He was respectful to all those He met. Those who were despised and hated, filthy and unclean, poor and ragged — He did not turn them away, but showed them mercy and compassion. Even those who spit upon Him and nailed Him to a cross were not exempt from His love and forgiveness.

Children learn by example. What does it say to them when they see me helping with the dishes, picking up the newspapers I have left on the floor and running the vacuum cleaner once in a while? It shows them that I have respect for the rest of the family. Respectful children come from respectful parents, and respectful parents are great parents.

Parenting Points:

❧ What things can you do this week to show respect for others in the home?

❧

❧

❧

❧

❧

Prayer:

Father God, help us begin to practice respect for each other in our home. Thank You for Your great example. May our children grow up respecting You and others because of our example. Amen.

$\mathcal{A}$ Love Note

*"Blessed are all who fear the Lord, who walk
in his ways . . . blessings and prosperity will be yours."*

A dear friend of mine recently received this note from her daughter who had been married only a few days. The wedding was a beautiful reflection of many years of a happy, healthy home. The letter read:

MOM,

Thanks *so* much for coming over a couple days to help me settle in. I really appreciated all your help in moving from your house to my new home. Thanks for being *so* upbeat and encouraging. I am so thankful for you. I appreciate your willingness to support me and help me out. Not many mothers would take their vacation days to help their daughter. But . . . *you* are always so willing. I appreciate you. Thanks also for treating Brian and me to meals while you were here. You and Dad are both so generous and giving to us. Who knows how we would be living without you guys?!

Thanks for your love. I am constantly amazed at what an awesome mom and dad I have. Both you and Dad mean *so* much to me. I am *so* blessed! Hope things went well for you this week!

Have a great time with Pops! Love, Jody

That's the kind of note I hope to receive in about twenty years. It reflects love, grace, nurture, care, trust — all the qualities of a true Christian home. That same daughter was a handful when she was little, but the commitment of her parents never wavered during the difficult times. Today, she is a beautiful young woman, full of poise and confidence.

My wife and I love being parents, but sometimes the days are exhausting. Raising children is often frustrating work, and not always do the parent magazines and scholarly journals give us the answers we need. It would be easy to just give up, sit back and let the children choose their own way, hoping that they will end up the way we want them to.

But the text for today gives us better advice, along with a promise. "Blessed are all who fear the Lord, who walk in his ways. You will eat the fruit of your labor; blessings and prosperity will be yours."

Doesn't that give you great hope? Isn't it wonderful to know that if we stand firm in our principles and follow the ways of the Lord, He will bless us and our children? The task might be overwhelming and the way might not seem clear, but God has promised us His strength and blessing.

Don't give up! Be steadfast and strong. And who knows — maybe you'll receive a love note from one of your children someday!

Parenting Points:

What are some things you appreciate about your own parents? Write them here.

If your parents are living, write them a letter, telling them of your love and appreciation.

Prayer:

God, thank You for the opportunity to teach our children about You and Your love. Help them to understand the decisions we make are for their own good. We want them to love You, even as we do. Amen.

Changing the Schedule

Theme:
The results of well-chosen priorities.
Text:
Matthew 28:20b

"And surely I am with you always, to the very end of the age."

During a flight from Atlanta to Grand Rapids, I sat across the aisle from a distinguished looking gentleman. As we began to talk about our jobs and our lives, our conversation turned to our children. It was then that I took the opportunity to tell him about my desire to teach and train my children in the ways of God.

He then shared with me this story: When his daughter was just a teenager, she won the leading role in her school play. He was so excited to think of his daughter on the stage — in the lights. His excitement quickly vanished after glancing at his calendar and realizing he had a commitment the same evening as opening night. It was a commitment that had been planned two years in advance. He had to decide what mattered most. In this case, he felt the school play deserved priority. After several phone calls and some rearranging of his schedule, he was free to attend the opening night. That evening he called his daughter in and shared how he had been able to change his schedule so he could be at her first performance.

The gentleman began to cry as he told me how she put her arms around his neck. I will always remember his next statement. He said, "As I reflect back, that moment changed our relationship. My daughter saw her significance in my life."

The Bible tells us plainly that we are God's highest priority. After all, He did send Jesus in order that we might have a personal relationship with Him. He held nothing back from us — not even the death of His own Son. And He did promise that He would always be with us, "even to the very end of the age."

Not always can we parents change our schedules in order to be with our children, but there ought to be some consideration in this area. How easy it is to let other events of significance crowd in and squeeze into a corner that which is the most important! We are so busy with our working lives that we often fail to pay attention to one of God's greatest gifts — our children.

What has highest significance in your life — your work or your children? Do they know how important they are to you? I challenge you today to look into your own schedule, rearrange your priorities, and get in touch with your little ones. You will never regret it.

Parenting Points:

Do you schedule regular times with your children?

Do you need to apologize to them for failing to attend a recent performance?

Develop some accountability in this area. Find someone who will help you guard your schedule.

Prayer:

Lord, thank You for promising to be with us always.
Give us guidance as we plan our schedules. Help us to keep eternity
in sight as we live each day. Bless our family with moments
of love and times of embracing each other. Amen.

How Many Is That?

Theme:
God's immeasurable love.
Text:
Psalm 57:10

"For great is your love, reaching to the heavens."

My three-year-old daughter, Cristina, was given a toy by her friend Brandon. He told her she could keep it for thirty days. All day she held that toy like it was gold, and even took it into the bathtub with her, and finally to bed. As I tucked her in, she said, "Dad, how many is thirty . . . is it all my fingers and all my toes?" I responded, "Well, it's all your fingers and all your toes and all my toes too!" She laughed her cute, cuddly laugh and replied, "That's a lot." We hugged and giggled as our heads huddled together on her pillow.

I am waiting for the day when Cristina asks me an even bigger question, "Dad, how much does God love me?" I want to help her understand that His love is immeasurable.

God's love cannot be defined by adding fingers and toes, or even by counting the stars in the sky. His love is so much greater than that.

Psalm 57:10 teaches us God's love reaches to the heavens. How much is that? Scientists have yet to find the point where the heavens end. They cannot be measured.

The greatest wonder of all is that this immeasurable love of God is a gift freely given to you and to me. There is nothing we can do to earn it or be worthy of it. His love goes before us and behind us, and nothing can separate us from it.

It is important that our children begin to learn about God's great love early in their lives, for it is the very foundation of our faith. What an awesome job for us parents — to teach our children about something so great it cannot be measured.

Parenting Points:

~&~ Begin counting your blessings. Share your list with your family.

~&~ Pray that your children will begin to understand God's love.

Prayer:

Lord, thank You for Your great love. Help us to grow in our understanding of its height, width and depth. Amen.

Mommy's the Best

Theme:
A godly wife and mother.
Text:
Proverbs 31:10

*"A wife of noble character who can find?
She is worth far more than rubies."*

Without question, one of the most effective ways parents can show love to their children is to show love to each other. Loving commitment seems to be vanishing from the families of today's society.

But love and commitment are still alive and well where they are sought with passion. A friend of mine gave his wife a love note — a paraphrase of Proverbs 31 — on Valentine's Day. I liked the idea so much I did it for my wife as well.

JANE
MY WIFE OF NOBLE CHARACTER

A wife of noble character I have found.
She is worth far more than rubies.
I have full confidence in her.
She brings me good, not harm, all the days of her life.
She selects clothing and other goods
And works with eager hands.
She tirelessly prepares food
And supplies the needs of her family.
She gets up while it is still early
To prepare for the waking of her children.
She is gifted with a business mind
And earns extra funds to provide little surprises for us.
She sets about her work vigorously
Her arms are strong for the tasks.
She is discerning with her expenditures,
Her family never fears for the necessities.

In her hands she holds the daily "to do" list
And goes about accomplishing those tasks each day.
She opens her arms to the poor
And extends her hands to the needy.
When it snows, she has no fear for her household,
For all of them are warmly clothed.
She makes bedspreads to cover our beds
And is clothed in eloquence.
Her example assures her husband is respected in society
And his opinions matter to the people.
She is clothed with strength and dignity,
She can laugh at the days to come.
She speaks with wisdom
And faithful instruction is on her tongue.
She watches over the affairs of the household
And does not eat the bread of idleness.
Her children arise and call her blessed,
Her husband also, and he praises her.
Many women do noble things,
But Jane, you surpass them all.
Charm is deceptive and beauty if fleeting,
But a woman who fears the Lord is to be praised.
Give her the reward she has earned,
Let her works bring her praise among the people.

Parenting Points:

Husbands, are you loving your wife as Christ loved the church — with sacrifice and selflessness?

Husbands, will your children look to you as an example of how to love a spouse?

Wives, could your husband lovingly and honestly give you this letter?

Wives, are you striving to improve in any of the areas mentioned in this Proverb? Which ones?

Prayer:

Lord, bless us as parents with a growing love for each other. Through the ups and downs of our own relationship, provide us with stability. We desire to be faithful to each other, just as You are faithful to us. Amen.

I Didn't Pick that Out!

Theme:
Dressing up in God's likeness.
Text:
Colossians 3:10

"Put on the new self, which is being renewed in knowledge in the image of its Creator."

An elementary school teacher was greeting her students as they entered the door to her classroom. As one little girl came into the room, the teacher noticed a sign attached to the back of her shirt. Upon closer inspection she read, "I hope you don't think I put together this outfit!"

I can imagine that distraught mother back at home, wondering if the teacher had seen it yet. I'm sure you've asked yourselves the same kinds of questions: "I wonder if they think I dress that way? They probably think I'm color-blind. I'm so embarrassed."

God must have days when He says, "I didn't pick that out for you today." When we put on our own selfish desires and dress in our own attitudes, we aren't leaving others with a good impression of God. They look at us and say, "If that's Christianity, then I want no part of it."

Chapter three of the book of Colossians provides rules for holy living. Verse three tells us to put on the *new* self — the one that reflects the knowledge and love of our Creator. The Apostle Paul wrote this to the church at Corinth: "Therefore, if anyone is in Christ, he is a new creation; the old has gone, the new has come!" (2 Cor. 5:17). Do you notice the emphasis on the word *new*? Just like we get rid of old garments that no longer fit us, so we must cast aside the old self and put on the newness of our life in Christ.

If we are not clothed in His likeness, it's time to enter His dressing room and begin the transformation.

Parenting Points:

꙾ Has God been pleased with your spiritual attire this week?

꙾ What could you take off and what could you put on to better reflect His image?

꙾ What are you doing to help your children learn to wear God's love?

Prayer:

Father God, thank You for supplying our needs of spiritual and physical clothing. Continue to renew us in our knowledge and understanding and image of You. Our family desires to reflect Your love today. Amen.

If You Do that One More Time

Theme:

Patience with the children.

Text:

Galatians 6:9

"Let us not become weary in doing good, for at the proper time we will reap a harvest if we do not give up."

When I was a boy, I often told myself I would never do some of the things to my children that my parents did to me. For instance, I would never make them brush their teeth before going to bed. I would never forbid cookies before supper. And I would never, never, never say "If you do that one more time . . ."

Here I am, now, with children of my own. And I have broken all of those promises I once made to myself — even the one about what I was never going to say. Why do parents always use that phrase? One would think we could come up with something a bit more original — that threat is as old as the hills.

I have been thinking about turning this phrase around to give it a positive connotation. What if we began to use this threat when we see our children doing something good? Suppose we said, "If I catch you doing that one more time, I'll take you out for pizza," what kind of response would there be? Or, "Do that again, and I'll pay you a dollar." What would our children do? Would they try to do that good deed again? Probably. Why? Because instead of threatening them when they are naughty, we are rewarding them for what they did right and encouraging them to continue on that path.

Our scripture for today says that we must not become weary in our efforts to do good, because someday we will be rewarded for our work. We must not become tired of praising our children, of coaxing them and encouraging them. We must continue to be supportive and loving and kind. We must never give up on them, for the day is coming when we will know that it was worth it all.

What a pity it is that so many parents are still caught in the old trap of harping on the mistakes and failures of their children instead of building up their good deeds and accomplishments. It is time for us to turn the saying around. Our children need to be encouraged today to do things that will enhance tomorrow in positive ways.

Parenting Points:

Does your home have more of a positive or a negative environment?

What can you do to focus more on the positive than the negative?

Prayer:

Lord, we commit ourselves to following Your guiding hand. Thank You for helping us deal with the frustrations of each day. You so freely forgive our areas of weakness, even when they become repetitive. Give us direction as we show that kind of love to our children. Amen.

Feed My Sheep

Theme:
A part of the flock.
Text:
Psalm 23

"The Lord is my shepherd . . . I shall not want."

Sometimes it seems like my wife and I are shepherds, herding a little flock of sheep — our children. We nudge them along, prodding them to get them moving. We bring them back when they go a little too far away. We provide for their needs and guide them along the right path. All this takes hard work and a lot of time, but we know that these little ones are our responsibility. We have a job to do, and we must not fail.

The Psalmist says that God is like a shepherd, caring for us, His little ones. How great it is to know that He is always with His flock and He will never grow tired of providing for our needs.

Find encouragement in this paraphrase of that Psalm.

A Parent's Psalm

The Lord is our Shepherd. My family will never lack for anything which we really need. He helps us enjoy our places of plenty. He provides restful, quiet surroundings. He guides us along the path of goodness.

Although we may walk through discouraging days — even to the point of death — we know that we need not fear, for He is with us. His shield of protection will guard us and His arms will embrace us and lift us to safety. He prepares a table of security in the midst of an unraveling society. He touches our souls and minds with healing; our cup of life overflows with joy.

Surely His goodness and love shall fill my house and remain with my children; and we will live with the Lord in heaven forever.

Parenting Points:

~ What "places of plenty" have you enjoyed as a family?

~ How have you seen God's "shield of protection" around your family?

~ What are three things you are currently doing to protect your family from Satan's attack?

~

~

~

Prayer:

Dear Shepherd, we praise You for life. Thank You for constantly walking with us; for bringing us rest and relaxation; for giving us new challenges every day. Continue to prepare tables before us as we seek Your Kingdom. Amen.

Living on Purpose

*"Before I formed you in the womb I knew you,
before you were born I set you apart."*

This notice appeared in the window of a coat store in Nottingham, England: "We have been established for over 100 years and have been pleasing and displeasing customers ever since. We have made money and lost money, suffered the effects of coal rationing, government control and bad payers. We have been cussed and discussed, messed about, lied to, held up, robbed and swindled. The only reason we stay in business is to see what happens next."

It is unfortunate that this seems to be the motto of many families. I watch some of my neighbors drive in and out of our cul-de-sac and I wonder at their aimlessness. They have no purpose, no plan, no destination. Their lives are filled with personal gain, selfish goals and temporary pleasures.

Our lives need purpose and direction. In the book of Jeremiah, we read of God's purpose for one man. God reassures Jeremiah that he is able to do the task set before him, even though it is monumental. He says, "Before I formed you in the womb I knew you, before you were born I set you apart; I appointed you as a prophet to the nations."

What a beautiful statement of purpose we see here. To be known by God, to be ordained to do His work — what could be more wonderful? And yet, that is the purpose for which God created all people. We are to love Him and serve Him and do His work. When our hearts are in tune with His desires, our lives gain significance and meaning. No longer must we come and go with no direction; we have a path to follow and a plan for life.

Most companies today have what is called a mission statement. It is a written declaration of that company's purpose and goals for the future. From time to time the company's directors will review the mission statement to see if anything needs to be changed or added. I think Christian families ought to develop mission statements as well. We ought to be continually reviewing our direction and goals, making sure that we are following our purpose — to do God's work.

God's plan for us can be overwhelming at times, just as it was for Jeremiah. He was not sure that he was qualified to do what God wanted him to do. Sometimes I feel that way as a parent. But God always reassures me that I can accomplish my goal, if only I keep His purpose before me and never waver from it.

Parenting Points:

Does your family have a statement of purpose? Write one today.

As parents, where do you often lose sight of your purpose?

Recognizing that God has a special plan for each of your children, what are you doing to develop that plan? List each child by name and respond.

Prayer:

God, continue to lay out Your purpose for our family. We commit ourselves to following You and accomplishing the tasks You set before us. We thank You for Your guidance and direction. We are Yours. Amen.

A Prayer a Day

Theme:
Guidance for daily prayers with our mate.
Text:
James 5:16

"The prayer of a righteous man is powerful and effective."

The Bible tells us that the earnest prayer of a righteous person is both powerful and effective. Often Jesus reminded His disciples to pray. In his letters to the churches, Paul writes about the importance of prayer. He says we are to never stop praying.

Several years ago, my wife and I began praying for each other and for our family on a daily basis. We have made this prayer time a special time of fellowship and communion together. It has been a most effective source of power and healing in our marriage. Here are some of the benefits we've discovered as a result of years of daily prayer together:

- By praying together, we are obeying God's command.
- Prayer creates unity in our marriage.
- Prayer unites our hearts in mutual concern for our children.
- As we communicate with our Lord, we improve our communication with each other.
- Prayer solidifies our love for each other.
- Uniting our hearts in prayer sets a good example for our children.
- When we pray, we put our marriage into God's hands.
- Prayer solves conflict.
- This daily fellowship enhances our physical intimacy.
- Daily prayer causes us to grow together spiritually.

Prayer has such healing power. It is difficult to remain angry when praying for someone. Prayer erases bitterness and hurt and allows the heart to be open to the love of God. Prayer can change the way we see each other, as we begin to look through Christ's eyes. Prayer can make a difference in the way we treat our children and our relatives. Most of all, prayer honors Christ and makes Him the center of our marriage.

Parenting Points:

Use these practical suggestions to help you begin praying together:

Establish a time for prayer. Stick to it.

Be consistent.

Read a portion of Scripture or a passage from a devotional book.

Focus your prayers on a different aspect of family life each day.

Husbands, you take the initiative to maintain this prayer time.

Prayer:

God, You desire our marriage to be the bond that holds our family together. Help us as we discipline ourselves to pray together each day. May our family be blessed because we have chosen to seek Your face. Amen.

If at First You Don't Succeed

Theme:
Teaching our children to win through failure.
Text:
Psalm 69:1-3

"Save me, O God, for the waters have come up to my neck. I sink in the miry depths, where there is no foothold. I have come into the deep waters; the floods engulf me. I am worn out calling for help; my throat is parched. My eyes fail, looking for my God."

One of the most difficult experiences of parenthood is watching our children face failure. Failure is difficult, whether it comes in the form of a poor test score, a fall off the bicycle or an umpire's "Strike three!"

The Psalmist was no stranger to pain and failure. Take note of his mounting problems in the scripture lesson for today: water up to his neck, no foothold to be found in the miry depths, flood waters all around, no help in sight. Can you relate? Of course you can! We all have been in this spot — where it seems like the world is caving in on us and there is no way out.

Don't give up hope. Our God has a way of turning our mistakes and failures around and making them into a source of learning. It is important for our children to learn that their mistakes are not the end of the world. Here are some practical hints to help make the way a bit easier.

When children fail:

~ Identify with them and share their pain.

~ Help them keep their failure in perspective.

~ Be willing to admit your own mistakes and grow with them.

~ Teach them that forgiveness doesn't eliminate pain, but gives hope.

~ Focus on what happens next.

Even though the Psalmist was weary and afraid of his failures, he still found a way to praise God. "I will praise God's name in song and glorify him with thanksgiving" (v. 30). We, too, can learn how to praise the Lord in the midst of failure. And with God's help, we can teach our children how to grow and become stronger by facing their own shortcomings and mistakes.

~ Parenting Points:

~ The next time you fail as a parent:

~ Ask God to forgive you. Ask forgiveness from the person or persons whom you have wronged.

~ Forgive yourself.

~ Model the way you want your children to handle failure.

~ Prayer:

Lord, thank You for forgiving our failures and for using them to help us mature in our faith. We pray that we will never fail You. Amen.

An Open Letter to Fathers

Theme:
Thoughts about a family man.
Text:
Matthew 12:33

"Make a tree good and its fruit will be good, or make a tree bad and its fruit will be bad, for a tree is recognized by its fruit."

A friend of mine recently shared with me a letter she wrote about men and their responsibilities in the home. It is a reflection of her family's thoughts about their dad.

Our youngest daughter was beautiful, with ocean-blue eyes and a tumble of tawny curls. At age three, she liked to climb into her dad's lap after a meal, snuggle up to his chest with a wide, satisfied smile, and purr, "Daddy, you're my safe place." And so he was, for all the members of his family.

Dads . . . husbands . . . in the eyes of your family, YOU are to be the "safe place" to go. You are our protector and provider. When you gather us together for a time with God, we need a "safe place." We need a "safe place", not a lecture about our shortcomings. A "safe place", not a sermon. We need a dad, a husband, who simply cares a lot about God and us. We don't need, or even want, a "spiritual giant". We just want you, as you are.

Your family needs a gathering time with God where it's safe to say to each other, "How are you and God getting along? Can we pray together?"

Your family needs a "safe place" to cry, laugh, sing, rejoice, challenge, share, confess, and sometimes just to keep quiet and have it okay. Your family needs time with you and God that's relaxed—unstiff, where we can pray honestly, in simple sentences, from our hearts. Unfixed. Unrigid. Unroutine. Unshackled. Real.

We, your family, need a "safe place" where irregular opinions are respected, and where God has the last word.

We need a gentleman leader, not a general. Gracious. Relaxed. Human. A family shepherd who exhibits not infallible authority, but authentic thirst for God.

Sit-down devotions every day? Not necessarily. Often? Yes. Long? Please, no! Formal? No. Where? Different places (be creative). How? Keep reading.

Dads, husbands, just try to sense where we're at, and zero in. We may need heavy-duty confessing to each other and God . . . or just silent prayer . . . or exuberant praise . . . or Bible study. But we don't need it all, every time.

Thanks for listening, fathers. We love you! Your family.

This is a good reminder for fathers. Keep focused on your responsibilities in life. If this letter brings to your attention some changes that need to be made in your life, then take the necessary steps that will set those changes in motion.

Christ loves us and desires us to grow. Many times He teaches us through those who love us most. Listen and learn.

Parenting Points:

Dads, allow each family member to share one area about you they appreciate and one area they would love to see you change. Listen . . . don't interrupt, thank them and close in prayer.

Prayer:

Lord, thank You for Your unconditional love and never ending grace. Help us to be the kind of parents we should be. May we always be looking for ways to improve our relationship with You. Amen.

Pre-op Moments

Theme:
Discovering Christ's peace in the midst of turmoil.
Text:
Colossians 3:15

"Let the peace of Christ rule in your hearts."

Our son, Alan, faced hernia surgery at the age of eight. The doctors had finished all the testing, and the day for the operation had finally arrived. My wife and I were as anxious as he was to put this surgery behind us and go home.

That Tuesday morning we were in the pre-operation area. The nurses had checked all his vital signs, and people in hospital garb had peeked at, poked and prodded every inch of his little body. As we continued to wait, my wife pulled out one of Alan's favorite books and began to read. I positioned myself against the wall and listened to her lovely voice. It was so peaceful and soothing that we became distracted from our troubles and lost track of why we were there in the first place.

When the doctor arrived to say it was time to go, Alan rubbed his eyes and said, "I was enjoying that so much I forgot where we were." The hospital staff wheeled him off as Jane and I chuckled about how caught up he was in the story. But the story had an effect on us as well, for a calm had settled over our anxious hearts and we were at peace during that difficult day. Certainly the Lord had visited us that morning.

Often the tension and pressure in our homes can build to a level that makes us restless and on edge. But if we take the time to listen, we can always find the calming voice of God, bringing His peace to us. Colossians 3:15 emphasizes, "Let the peace of Christ rule in your hearts, since as members of one body you were called to peace. And be thankful."

How thankful I am for His peace! To know that He is with me in all the big and little anxieties of my life, calming my fears — this is too wonderful for words.

Parenting Points:

~ Who creates the most tension in your home?

~ What steps can be taken to help eliminate some of the tension?

~ What situation looms before you today? Will you remember to look for God's peace?

Prayer:

*Lord, rule in our hearts and bring peace to our home.
May Your name be glorified in our lives, even through times of
difficulty and anxiety. Help us to rely on You for our strength,
and we will continue to be thankful. Amen.*

You're Gonna Get a Spanking

Theme:
Putting the emphasis on the wrong end.
Text:
Psalm 127:1

"Unless the Lord builds the house, its builders labor in vain."

Do you remember getting spanked when you were a child? What was your reaction? Mine was usually to kick the dog or ram my fist into the wall. I recall once sticking out my tongue at Mom as she walked away after a spanking. She turned a bit quicker than I anticipated and we had the opportunity to go through the process again.

Our children respond to us, too, after moments of physical discipline. Who knows what goes on after we leave the room? I am discovering that discipline is not only a physical activity, but a spiritual and mental one as well. One of life's lessons taught me a new approach.

It was a hot, muggy day in July, and the boys were helping me hang some doors on hinges after a recent move to a new home. We began our work early to beat the heat, but by mid-morning we were all getting a bit sweaty. As we carried each door into the house, one of the children would pray that it would fit and be easy to hang. Prayer works . . . everything was going smoothly.

An interruption drew the boys outside and I continued to carry doors in by myself. One door was particularly contrary. No matter how much I sawed, scraped, sanded or yelled, it was still stuck. I finally ripped off enough wood to make it fit, and went on to the next one. It was ten times worse than the one before. I was getting frustrated.

Suddenly it occurred to me that we had ceased praying and I was trying to do the work on my own, without God's help. I called the boys in and asked them to pray with me for the remaining doors. Wouldn't you know it, every one fit perfectly! The children threw their hands in the air and yelled, "Way to go, God!"

The Lord began to speak to me about how I discipline my family. He brought before me this verse, "Unless the Lord builds the house, its builders labor in vain." Many times I try to be the one to provide all the answers to family conflicts, but this verse teaches me that I am incapable. I can sand, scrape, saw, strip and yell, but without the power of the Master Builder, my structure will crumble.

How, then, should we discipline? How do we keep from focusing on the wrong end — the physical? We must teach our children the right way and pray for them daily. Teaching and praying — without them, discipline is only a spanking. With a balanced approach, God can do more than we imagine.

Parenting Points:

Do you pray for your children daily?

What can you do to change your approach to discipline?

Prayer:

Lord, unless we have Your strength, we are incapable of being the kind of parents You want us to be. Help us to let go and allow You to have Your way in our family. Thank You for Your care. Amen.

It's Your Serve

"Lord, are you going to wash my feet?"

Often throughout Christ's ministry, He gathered His disciples together for a time of teaching and special fellowship. This particular occasion was especially significant, because in just a few hours He would be crucified. Even though the disciples did not understand right away what Jesus was doing, it became a memory that would forever be etched in their minds.

In Christ's day, the roads throughout Palestine were dry and dusty. When the rains came, they turned into seas of mud. As travelers walked along these roads, their feet and sandals became very dirty. Each homeowner would put a basin of cool water near the door of his house, and as the guests arrived, servants would wash their hot, dusty feet.

As the disciples assembled, there was probably some question as to who should take on the role of servant and wash the others' feet. No one was willing to stoop to that level. Then Jesus took off His outer garment and wrapped a towel around His waist. Picking up the basin of water, He proceeded to bathe the tired feet of His friends.

They were shocked at His actions! Why was the Messiah, their Lord and Master, assuming the responsibilities of a servant? Jesus was teaching them that true greatness begins with servanthood. When Peter began to understand, He said, "Christ, not just my feet, but wash my whole self."

Serving others is so uncommon in our day. We watch basketball players toss their warm-ups on the floor and a "servant" folds them and prepares them to be used again. Politicians are catered to on every corner. Professional businessmen use expense accounts to live luxurious lives. The competition to impress others seems to be building on every side. And in the middle of this competitive war, Christ asks us to "wash each others' feet."

When was the last time we took time to serve someone in our family? I believe that servanthood in the home begins with the father. I must ask myself continually, Am I an example of servanthood? Do my children see me helping my wife and putting her first, before my own needs? Are they learning from me what it means to serve others? If not, then I need to discover the joy of serving in my home. What a difference having the heart of a servant can make!

Parenting Points:

In what ways do the members of your family serve each other?

Dad:

Mom:

Children:

How could your family be a better example of servanthood in your neighborhood?

Prayer:

Lord help us to practice serving each other at home so our light will shine even more effectively for You in the world. Bless our family with caring, sharing spirits. May we never forget Your example. In Your name, Amen.

Twinkle, Twinkle, Little Star

Theme:
The importance of memorizing scripture.

Text:
Psalm 119:11

"I have hidden your word in my heart that I might not sin against you."

My children love to sing. I finally figured out that combining familiar songs with Bible verses would be a good way to memorize scripture. So we tried it. It was simple, and the children thought it was great.

I've heard them singing those verses during their playtime. As their childish voices fill the air with the Word of God, I am reminded of the Psalmist's words: "I have hidden your word in my heart that I might not sin against you."

Christ often quoted the prophets in His answers to the disciples and the Pharisees, and even to Satan himself. These statements were no doubt verses that He had memorized during those early, growing years. He had heard them so many times that they had become a part of Him. When called upon to make a decision, He was ready because He had hidden God's Word in His heart.

How will God's Word help our children? By planting His Word in their hearts, we give them a foundation for their faith. His Word tells them how to live, how to treat others and where to turn in times of need. It reassures them of His love and calls them to follow His example. His Word is eternal and unchanging. It is always relevant and always true. Is there anything else in life that can be described this way?

The memory verses my daughter sings today might be the words she needs to recall some night on a steamy date or in making an important decision in life. My goal is to teach eternal truths in any way I can, so that when the time comes, her answer will be strong and sure.

Parenting Points:

- Select a favorite scripture verse and match it up with one of these tunes. Keep singing it until the whole family memorizes it. Let them join in and create some more songs!
  - Twinkle, Twinkle Little Star

  - Mary Had a Little Lamb

  - Row, Row, Row Your Boat

  - Any other childhood tunes you know.

- How many scriptures have you memorized related to parenting? Where are you looking for help in the parenting decisions you must make?

Prayer:

Lord, teach our family the value of memorizing the truth of the Bible. Thank you for giving us Your Word that never changes. Help us to practice these truths in front of our children and with each other. Amen.

Play Pretties

Theme:
Our hidden potential vs the visible mess
Text:
Genesis 1:27

"God created man in His own image."

The house appeared to have been struck by a tornado. Play cups, saucers and utensils were everywhere. Not a toy appeared to be in its proper place. Two people walked into this scenario at the same time but had very different reactions. Mother spoke first. "What is going on here? Who made this mess? What have you done to my favorite scarf?" Grandma offered a different point of view. "Look at all the beautiful play pretties scattered here and there. Isn't it beautiful?" Same room, same toys, but different perspectives.

Sometimes we parents expect the worst from our children, and usually we get just what we expect. Occasionally, it might be of benefit to look beyond the mess and see the potential lying within.

I recently read about an artist who, as a child, had been left with the responsibility of watching his younger sister while his mother went out to shop for groceries. While she was gone, the young Picasso took out his brushes and supplies and began to paint a picture of his sister. He painted several spots on the rug, too, as well as a few on the wall. When his mother came home, she ignored the mess and focused on the painting. "Oh what a beautiful painting," she proclaimed as she kissed her son lightly on the forehead. The artist later said, "God gave me the talent, but my mother gave me the wings to fly."

God sees potential in us. He says that we are made in His likeness. Even when I fail to maintain the beauty of that image and make a mess of things, He lifts me up and encourages me to keep going. He tells me of His love for me and reminds me of my great worth in His eyes.

I want to be the kind of parent that sees past the toys that lie on the floor to the joy and creativity that lie in the hearts of my children. I want to play with them, laugh with them and encourage them to be all they can be.

Parenting Points:

Pour a bucket of building blocks or the pieces of a puzzle onto the floor tonight and invite the children to come play with you.

What potential do you see in your children? List them here.

Name:	Name:	Name:

Prayer:

Lord, You've blessed us with wonderful children.
There are times when we don't enjoy them because we're
too focused on keeping the house perfect. Help us to see their
potential, even as You see potential in us. Amen.

Temperature 104.5

Theme:
A solution for panic situations.
Text:
2 Chronicles 20

"We do not know what to do, but our eyes are on You."

Do you ever panic? I know, that was a stupid question to ask of a parent. The fact is, there are many times during the course of raising children when panic sets in. Every parent knows what I'm talking about.

Of course, there are different levels of parental panic. There's the panic you feel when you are startled by a loud noise in the next room and you wonder if someone is hurt. There's the panic that comes in the middle of the night, when your child has a temperature of 104 degrees and nothing seems to work to bring it down. And then, there's the panic that grabs you and seems to suffocate you in its stranglehold. This usually happens when blood is visible and the number 911 is running through your head.

King Jehoshaphat found himself in a panic situation. He had just been told about a big army secretly making its way into his territory, ready to attack. Jehoshaphat was alarmed. It was panic time. But what did Jehoshaphat do? Did he run this way and that, screaming and making a spectacle? No! The Bible tells us that Jehoshaphat stood before the Lord in the presence of all the people of Judah. And he petitioned the Lord on behalf of his nation. He sought God first — before panic could take over.

I can learn a lesson from Jehoshaphat. I must confess, I usually try every other way possible before I think about turning to the Lord. I need to follow Jehoshaphat's example and gather my family around me in times of crisis, so that we may approach the Lord together and ask for His blessing and protection. And then I need to get in touch with others who are willing to go before the Lord on my behalf.

Prayer is the greatest antidote for panic. It is difficult to panic when in the presence of the Almighty, for His peace washes away my fears and give me hope.

Parenting Points:

What do you normally do in moments of panic?

Are there people praying for you? Who can you call to support you when life's crises come?

Prayer:

Lord, we realize there will be many times of panic in our lifetime. Help us to remember to seek You first. We trust in You for all of life that is yet to come. Amen.

Honey, I Shrunk the Kids

Theme:
Belief in your children.
Text:
Genesis 22:12

"Now I know that you fear God because you have not withheld from me your son, your only son."

There is nothing quite so beautiful as parents who praise and encourage their children. I sat beside a family at an elementary school Christmas program not long ago and was thoroughly blessed by their show of love and support.

From the amount of video equipment set up around them, it was obvious that some member of their family was about to perform the most important role of a lifetime. The grandmother leaned over to me, and, pointing to her program, said, "That little boy is my grandson." I attempted to act surprised and encouraged her to take the lens cap off her camera. Their little actor finally entered stage left and shared ten words while the whole family held their breath. When he finished, they laughed, hugged and cheered so much they missed seeing the next speaker.

And then my son was on stage. He didn't have any solo parts, but he sure did look awesome. I was certain that every parent out there was looking right at him, wishing he was theirs. As I looked around at other parents, I noticed many smiling their encouragement for their own children.

Suddenly I began to think about other children on that stage — those who had no one there to believe in them. While so many were growing in confidence, they were shrinking, losing belief in themselves.

Genesis 22 records one of the most treasured stories in the Bible.

The picture of Isaac on the altar is worth more than words can say. Isaac respected his father, understood his own self-worth and knew that God had a bigger plan. It was obvious that he had known years of support and encouragement from a loving family.

We only have a little time to build self-worth and confidence in our children. Let's do everything we can to help them grow into adults who believe in themselves.

Parenting Points:

What can you do to build your children's belief in themselves?

With the help of your children, select a child in the neighborhood who has unsupportive parents and begin to encourage and support him. See what a difference you can make in one life.

Prayer:

Lord, in You we find our self-worth. Continue to use us as tools to build up our children and strengthen them as individuals. Help us in our goal to reach others in our neighborhood for You. Amen.

Discover Watts New

Theme:
The intensity of our spiritual brightness.
Text:
Matthew 5:14-16

"You are the light of the world."

I don't know a lot about light bulbs. I don't understand how electricity works or how the filament inside of the bulb is made. When we run out, I go to the store and buy more — usually the discounted ones. Then I have to make a decision. What wattage should I buy? I do know this much — there is a big difference between a 40-watt and a 100-watt bulb.

Our family's witness for Christ can be compared to the output of an electric light bulb. Sometimes we are a 40-watt family. The lights of joy and happiness are flickering on and off. We are not giving off the kind of glow that would draw others to us, and ultimately, to Jesus Christ. Other times we are more like 60-watt bulbs. We shed enough light to make a statement about our faith, but not enough to reach out into the dark corners of our neighborhood.

God wants us to shine like 100-watt bulbs — radiating out into the darkness and shedding light on all those around us. This kind of Christianity cannot be contained or stifled. It continues to shine, touching lives and changing the world.

In the Sermon on the Mount, Jesus says these words: "You are the light of the world . . . . Let your light shine before men, that they may see your good deeds and praise your Father in heaven."

What happens when the light is turned on? The shadows melt away, our fears of the dark subside, we feel safer and more confident. Showing the love of Christ to others is like turning on a light bulb in a dark room. Jesus tells us in John 8:12, "Whoever follows me will never walk in darkness, but will have the light of life."

God needs us to bring His light into a dark and hurting world. Look around you. There are people everywhere in need of the Savior and His life-changing grace. You have the light. Let it shine!

Parenting Points:

❧ Together with your children, put a 40, 60, 75 and 100-watt bulb into a lamp and discuss the brilliance of each. Talk about how the whole family can shine brightly for Christ at home and in the neighborhood.

❧ How brightly do you shine in front of your children? What can you do to develop more brilliance?

Prayer:

Lord, thank You for the light You have given us. Shine through us that we may make a difference in our home and in our neighborhood. May we always be reflections of Your love. Amen.

I've Still Got You

Theme:
Trust in God when you're teetering.
Text:
Psalm 37:24

"Though he stumble, he will not fall, for the Lord upholds him with his hand."

Joshua and I took off the training wheels together. As we worked, I said all those things a father is supposed to say on such an occasion. "Always keep pedaling. Turn the handlebars in the direction you are teetering. Pedal backwards to stop. Don't look back at me. Stay focused."

So with all the bolts and training wheels on the asphalt, we headed for a flat surface. I ran along beside the bike, holding onto the back of the seat and yelling directions. Up and down the street we teetered, sometimes going four or five feet without my hand on the seat. The neighbors added their encouragement. "You're doing great Josh. Keep trying. Don't give up." He didn't. Several times we had to stop and start over. Finally, when my bare feet had had enough, we quit for the day. Josh's face was shining. "I love this, Dad. Tomorrow I'll do it all by myself."

As I thought about Josh's accomplishment that day, I realized that the reason for his success was my steadying hand on the seat of his bike. He knew I was right there beside him. He trusted me to steady the bike and keep it from falling. The knowledge that I would not leave him or let him fall gave him the courage to keep pedaling.

Our Heavenly Father reaches out His steadying hand of love to us. His Word tells us that even though we may stumble, we will not fall, for the Lord holds us with His hand. When we can rest in the knowledge of His presence and trust in His guiding hand — only then will we have the courage and strength to carry on through the difficult moments in life.

Our families will encounter many ups and downs. But the steady hand of the Lord will never change. His promise is sure and His love will last forever.

Parenting Points:

✒ Can you recall several times when God's protection has been evident in your life?

✒ Thank God for being with you through each of those times.

✒ What are you doing to help your children keep balance in their lives?

Prayer:

Lord, thank You for holding us in Your hand and steadying us through the ups and downs of life. Teach us to trust You more and help us grow in our knowledge of You. Amen.

Are We There Yet?

Theme:
God's gentle pruning.
Text:
John 15:1-8

"Every branch that does bear fruit he prunes so that it will be even more fruitful."

According to the manager of a California vineyard, there are several secrets to a quality crop. Every good gardner knows that no two vines are identical. Each one must be pruned differently. How old is the vine? How is the vine supported — on its own, or on a stake? Does it get the hot afternoon sun or only the cooler rays? Is it in vigorous health, and should its crop be retained this year or sacrificed for the future good of the vine? Where on the vine should spurs be permitted to grow? A master pruner must know all such things and care for each vine according to its own individual needs.

Our Heavenly Father cares for us in much the same way. He looks at our personalities, our needs, our abilities and our circumstances, and He gently prunes us so that we will produce a great harvest for His kingdom. He cuts away those attitudes and actions that do not reflect His image and trims off the thoughts and words that do not honor His name. Sometimes this process can be painful, but it is necessary if we are to become like Him.

Likewise, we must be concerned with the raising of our children. Without pruning, they would grow wild and unproductive. Many questions come to my mind. Do I recognize the uniqueness of each one of my children? Am I remembering their ages and personalities as I discipline them and train the light of God to shine into their hearts? Am

I a good example of what I want them to be?

If our families are going to be productive for Christ, we need to experience this growth together. Cutting, pruning, rebudding — it's all part of God's plan. Are we there yet? No, but in giving ourselves to the Master Pruner, we know that we are closer every day.

Parenting Points:

🌿 Take time to answer the questions listed in the paragraph above.

🌿 In what area is God pruning you and your spouse for greater effectiveness in your marriage and in your parenting?

Prayer:

Lord of the harvest, since You know what is best for us, we want You to do with us what You will. Change us and help us to grow, that we may bear fruit for You. Amen.

Temper, Temper, Temper!

Theme:
An antidote for anger.

Text:
Psalm 145:8

*"The Lord is gracious and compassionate,
slow to anger and rich in love."*

The checkout line had been moving at a snail's pace and finally came to a complete stop. The cashier held a phone to each ear. She appeared to be talking with people who were unable to solve the problem. Another checkout register opened, so we pulled our loaded cart to the new lane and waited. A new complication arose with this newly opened register, so we were instructed to go to yet another lane. During all this watching and waiting, a young lady huffed and puffed, expressing her dissatisfaction with the whole scene. As the line shifted to the new lane, she squeezed herself in front of us and plopped her items on the checkout counter. We made no strong objection to this; however, the cashier deemed it unfair and proceeded to check out our items first. This was not a good idea! The dissatisfied customer grabbed some of our grocery items from our cart and literally threw them on the counter, proclaiming loudly, "Here's some of their junk!"

I calmly told the lady I was sorry if we had inconvenienced her, all the while keeping my wide-eyed children snuggled around me as the cashier kept on with her duties. The irritated lady continued to become angrier still, until finally I asked the cashier to zero our total and please serve the lady before finishing our order. Again the cashier insisted on helping us first.

Not knowing what else to do, I turned to the angry customer and said, "What would you like me to do?" She loudly replied, "Just SHUT-UP!" I did not know what to do or say. I chose to ignore her while we finished our transaction.

As soon as we walked out of the store, the children found their voices. "Dad, she was rude." "I think she got up on the wrong side of the bed." "What a rotten attitude!" What a golden teaching opportunity this was turning out to be! "Children," I said, "remember what you saw in there. Don't ever act in such a way that others will be able to say those kinds of things about you." That night at bedtime, we asked God to somehow help her deal with her anger and open her heart to His love.

Anger exists in many of our homes. Parents who have not learned how to deal with their anger often take it out on their spouses or children. Anger drives thousands of couples to divorce each year and tears apart hundreds of families each day. Note what the Psalmist tells us about God: "He is gracious and compassionate, slow to anger and rich in love."

These four adjectives — gracious, compassionate, slow to anger, rich in love — are words that should describe us as well. Families that imitate Christ are those that will stand firm.

Parenting Points:

How would you rate yourself in graciousness, compassion, slowness to anger, and richness in love?

Establish accountability between you and your spouse to help you control your tempers in the home.

Prayer:

Lord, thank You for your graciousness and compassion.
Help us learn to exercise self-control, that we may become
more like You. Bless our home with love. Amen.

A Father's Dream

Theme:
The best way to be remembered.
Text:
Deuteronomy 6:5-9

"These commandments that I give you today are to be upon your hearts. Impress them on your children."

My friend, Doug, had a wonderful experience on Fathers Day. His three daughters decided to write him notes of appreciation, and each one created a unique refrigerator masterpiece to add to the decor of their kitchen. His 10 year-old daughter, Emily, gave him a "Top Ten" list of how she will remember him:

1. A big-time golfer!
2. Family always first!
3. Always there for hard math problems.
4. Took us out for ice cream sundaes.
5. Made sure we had family devotions.
6. Always bought unneeded grocery items!
7. Fished with me.
8. Hard worker.
9. Taught sports to us.
10. Did dirty, stinky jobs around the house!
11. Never missed a promised date!

That is without a doubt the best list I have ever seen. Did you notice that Emily had so many good things to say about her dad that she couldn't keep her list to ten items? What does it take to be the kind of father who inspires such love and devotion?

We find the answer in our scripture for today. God tells His people that the most important thing in the world is to love the Lord and keep His commandments. Then, we must teach our children what we know of God's love. How must we teach? By word and example.

Dads, are you dreaming of the day when you will receive a list of loving attributes from your children? Start now by teaching them the ways of the Lord. Show them His love in the way you spend time with them. Make sure that they know, every day, of your unconditional love for them. Your children will forever be grateful.

Parenting Points:

❧ Ask your children to tell you the things they will always remember about you.

❧ List some ways you want your children to remember you.

❧ Read "7 *Things Kids Never Forget*" by Ron Rose (1993: Questar Publishers Inc.)

Prayer:

Lord, thank You for being our Lord and Savior.
Help us as we teach our children Your ways and show
them Your love. Continue to bless us with Your grace today. Amen.

Don't Rush It

Theme:
Enjoy every stage of parenting.

Text:
Philippians 4:11-12

"I have learned the secret of being content in any and every situation."

Take a moment to look at pictures of your children when they were babies. Do you remember the joy of those early years? Do you remember the first smile, the first step, the first time she said "Da-da?" Do you also remember the dirty diapers, spilled formula and sleepless nights? I do. And I recall wishing and praying for the next stage of parenthood.

But the next stage brings its own problems. Dirty diapers give way to school issues, and suddenly we're dealing with drivers' licenses, dating, and then, empty nests. Oh, how quickly our lives pass, and how often we fail to enjoy the moment that is before us.

Learning the secret of enjoying each day is an art. Those who master it have a bigger understanding of life. Take it from those who've traveled the road — slow down and enjoy the show.

Paul teaches in Philippians 4:11-12 that there is contentment to be found in Christ in all circumstances. We can learn to be happy when we are in need or when we are blessed with plenty, when we are fed or when we are hungry. We can find contentment when we are surrounded by dirty diapers and runny noses or when the children are sleeping soundly. We can be happy in life no matter what the circumstances. We do not always need to be looking for something else, hoping that the next stage will better than this one.

Moms and Dads, determine now to slow down and enjoy every minute of the time God gives you with your children. All too soon they will be gone and your house will no longer ring with their noise and laughter. Set aside the dirty dishes to play a game with them. Encourage their creativity. Laugh at their jokes. You will never be sorry, for you will be rewarded with great contentment.

Parenting Points:

How often do you find yourself looking to the next stage of parenting instead of being content with the present?

What are your children doing now that deserves a family celebration?

Make a commitment to remind each other to celebrate each day of life.

Prayer:

Lord, You have promised today, not tomorrow.
Give us contentment that we may enjoy each stage of parenting.
Thank You for Your gracious gift of today. Amen.

101 Ways To Improve At Dadhood!

*Practical Ways For
Fathers To Grow Up With Their Children.*

Dan Seaborn

Being a dad is in! From learning to spend quality time with their kids to spending more time on their knees, dads are "coming out of the closet" and accepting their responsibilities. The purpose of this book is to provide some practical ideas for growing in your relationship with your children. Some of the ideas will be fun, others will require a time of internal inspection.

Thanks for joining me in this movement to restore the joy and blessing of family life to our homes, our neighborhoods and our world.

– Dan Seaborn

101 Ways To Love Your Wife

*"Fresh, innovative, practical ideas
for helpless husbands."*

Dan Seaborn

Most men *believe* they are to care for
the emotional needs of their wife.

Few Do!

Most men *want to* have fun and be
creative in their marriage relationship.

Few Know How!
